FLORIDA'S HISTORIC RESTAURANTS

and their recipes

JOHN F. BLAIR, Publisher
Winston-Salem, North Carolina

FLORIDA'S HISTORIC RESTAURANTS

and their recipes

**by DAWN O'BRIEN
and BECKY ROPER MATKOV**

Drawings by Debra L. Hampton

Library of Congress Cataloging-in-Publication Data

O'Brien, Dawn.
Florida's historic restaurants and their recipes/by Dawn O'Brien
and Becky Matkov; drawings by Debra L. Hampton.

p.   cm.
Includes index.
ISBN 0-89587-057-6   : $12.95
1. Cookery, American—Southern style.   2. Cookery—Florida.
3. Restaurants, lunch rooms, etc.—Florida—Guide-books.
4. Historic buildings—Florida.   I. Matkov, Becky.   II. Title.
TX715.02827 1987   87-26540
641.509759—dc19   CIP

iv

DEDICATION

My part of this book is dedicated to Joseph Collins, who believes that young women deserve an education too.
  Dawn O'Brien

To my friends across the state of Florida who have shared their personal recommendations and dining experiences with me; to my husband, Tom, for his support all these years; to my son, Tom, and my daughter, Grimsley, for surviving yet another of their mother's whirlwind projects.
  Becky Roper Matkov

ACKNOWLEDGMENTS Florida has offered a whole spectrum in historic restaurant research. The state that people think of as "variety vacation land" has not taken a vacation from preserving its past. There were many devoted native and adopted Floridians who uncovered paths for us during the researching and writing of this book that otherwise would have been difficult to find. To those people we owe a special debt of thanks. A big thank you to the following:

To: Catherine Haagenson, Manager of Domestic Publicity for the Florida Department of Commerce in the Division of Tourism, and Jan Tully, Information Officer for the division.

To: The Florida county tourism development councils, chambers of commerce and promotion agencies, especially to Leah Hamm, Jan Higginbotham, Royce Hodge, Janette Hunt, Larry Marthaler, Nancy McWilliams and Gary Stogner.

To: The Florida Trust for Historic Preservation, especially Mary Barrow, Jean Bunch, Bud Frazier, Sallye Jude, Tavia McCuean and Ralph Renick.

To: Florida Historic Preservation Advisory Council, especially Katharine Dickenson, Joan Jennewein, Roy Hunt, Marcia Lindstrom and Don Slesnick.

To: Tampa Preservation, Inc., especially Frances Kruse and Harriet Plyler.

To: Dade Heritage Trust, especially Tom Collins, Nancy Leibman, Joan Miller and Margo Newton.

To: The Historic Preservation Committee of the Junior League of Miami, Inc., especially Liz Bishop and Anna Ehlert.

To: Leslie Rivera of the Vizcayan Foundation.

To: Allison DeFoor of the Florida Keys Land Trust.

To: Bill Branan of Florida Defenders of the Environment.

To: George Sandora of the Gallery at Cedar Key.

To: Bob Jensen of the Elizabeth Ordway Dunn Foundation.

To: Professor Blair Reeves of the University of Florida School of Architecture.

To: Herb Hiller, author of the *Guide to the Small and Historic Lodgings of Florida*.

To: Arlene Commings of the Florida Main Street Program, Sebring.

To: Cookie O'Brien of the St. Augustine Historic Preservation Board.

To: Sherry Davich of Orlando Landmarks Defense Inc.

To: Leadership Florida Network members: Rick Edmonds and Geoffrey Simon.

To: Gloria Anderson of *Miami Today* newspaper.

To: The restaurateurs, who shared their restaurants' heritage, and the chefs who shared their time and talents.

To: The artist, Debra Hampton, for such beautiful renderings.

To: The many guinea pigs who continue to taste and appreciate each state's culinary benefits.

FOREWORD "Let them eat pizza!" was my collaborator Becky Roper Matkov's terse comment when her teen-age son Tom sat down to a delectable meal that she had spent hours perfecting, and after one bite announced, "Not bad, Mom. Now this is the kind of stuff Rob's live-in maid cooks every night—only she doesn't make such a mess in the kitchen."

I could sympathize. Six years ago, when I began the first of now seven books on historic restaurants, that was the same type of "encouraging" dig my then teen-age daughter Daintry delivered at our table.

What did I do? Because Daintry was a good driver and a photographer, I started taking her with me to the restaurants when school schedules permitted. Little by little, she and her sister Shannon Heather began not only to develop an appreciation for unusual and simply prepared food, but to gain a sense of history. As they listened to the stories and saw the quality of craftsmanship in these buildings, they began to understand the importance of preserving them. Listening to the pride of the preservationists, who undertook the research and often spent long hours in tedious, backbreaking work, made an impression on my daughters. This impression was underscored further in our kitchen, where they were called on to stir this or measure that.

Admittedly, the original reason I sought out restaurants in restored buildings was to record their stories. I wanted that kinship with the past. From the beginning, Becky's main interest in the project lay in having the opportunity to spotlight her favorite subject, "interesting old buildings being preserved and restored and used in economically viable ways."

We have discovered that our nation's history is unveiled in places that range from the simple and unpretentious to the glamorous and opulent. Yet each building, being a minimum of fifty years old (a part of the criteria used for the National Register of Historic Places), has defined our heritage in a multitude of ways. Many of the buildings were private homes whose occupants have added interesting footnotes to the daily life of that period. Others have served as a school, retail store, hospital, houseboat—even a rabbit hutch. We've seen the influences of many ethnic regions and celebrate the new foods that have been introduced to our palates.

What I think is important here is not just that Becky and I are cheerleaders for the preservationists or the restaurateurs; the value lies in awakening a comprehension in our society (and our children) that one of the purposes of restoration is to bring the thing that is restored back into the mainstream. And there is nothing more in the current mainstream than the superb food found in the historic restaurants featured here. Add to this the fact that we were able to reproduce their recipes in our kitchens, and our project, this book and the others in the series, has a real *raison d'être*.

The best news to my ears is, as Becky says, "More historic restaurants are opening every day. This is being made possible, in part, by historic preservation tax incentives that encourage developers to rehabilitate, rather than destroy." For us it also created a pleasant problem—there were far more than fifty eligible restaurants from which to choose. Your favorite restaurant might not have made this printing due to that problem, and for these "sins of omission" we apologize.

We hope this book helps guide our readers to many pleasant dining experiences in those restaurants that preserve our heritage and give us a pride in our past.

CONTENTS

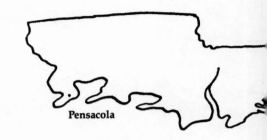

Pensacola

• Tallahassee
• Wakulla Springs

Fernandina Beach

St. Augustine

High Springs •
Gainesville •
Ocala •

Mount Dora •
Winter Park •
Orlando •

Cedar Key

• Lakeland
• Tampa   • Lake Wales

Clearwater
St. Petersburg Beach

• Sarasota

Palm Beach

Boca Raton
Lighthouse Point

Bokeelia
Captiva Island   • Fort Myers

Fort Lauderdale
Miami Beach

Fort Myers Beach

Miami
Coral Gables

Goulds •

Key West

SCOTTO'S RISTORANTE ITALIANO
Pensacola

SCOTTO'S RISTORANTE ITALIANO

In 1752, Spanish colonists established Pensacola as a permanent settlement near present-day Seville Square. Today, this area is a lively center of restoration work, with many eighteenth- and nineteenth-century cottages and mansions being turned into shops and galleries. The heart of the Seville Historic District is Seville Square, a public park used for festivals, art shows and other special events.

Overlooking this square is Scotto's Ristorante Italiano, located in a charming one-story house built in the 1880s. The brown frame building, with a hip roof, is accented with white gingerbread trim on the front porch and dark brown shutters. The structure for many years was the home of the Jazz Musicians Union.

The restaurant is owned by Richard Scotto and his wife Pat. Family portraits of the Scotto family are spotlighted on the walls. One is of Genaro and Lucia shortly after their arrival from Italy's Isle of Capri. Another is of Richard's father, "Pappa Joe," in the 1920s; this picture became the basis for the restaurant's logo.

The Scotto men have always been the cooks in the family, founding the Premiere Bakery in Pensacola in 1945. Grandfather Genaro taught son Guiseppe treasured family recipes, and now grandson Richard carries on the tradition as he prepares classic—and exceptional—Italian masterpieces.

To Pat Scotto fell the task of decorating the restaurant, which she did in soothing colors of pink and green, applying stenciling to the walls herself. She also manages up front and has the pleasant job of being official taste tester.

This is a duty I envy after my own sampling of some of their delectable dishes. Their menu selections feature everything from Fettucine Scotto, made with crabmeat and shrimp, to Veal Marsala and Chicken Cacciatora. They make their own pasta daily, and all ingredients are fresh.

The Ravioli with Italian Sausage, served with a tangy tomato sauce, was delicious, as was the Red Fettucine. I also tried the Stuffed Eggplant with Crabmeat, and it was fabu-

2

lous. "Richard's Famous Homemade Cheesecake" lived up to its reputation. And my own reputation as a cook wasn't harmed a bit when I tried Richard's recipe out at home.

Just add their authentic Italian music to their Italian food, and you have a romantic evening worthy of the Riviera.—B.R.M.

Scotto's Ristorante Italiano is located at 300 South Alcaniz Street in Pensacola. Lunch is served from 11:00 a.m. to 2:00 p.m. Monday through Friday. Dinner is served from 5:00 to 10:00 p.m. Monday through Saturday. Reservations are recommended; call (904) 434-1932.

SCOTTO'S RISTORANTE ITALIANO'S
STUFFED EGGPLANT

4 medium-size eggplants
3 celery stalks, diced
1 onion, chopped
1 green bell pepper, diced
1 red bell pepper, diced
2 teaspoons chopped fresh
  garlic
2 tablespoons butter
4 ounces olive oil
1 cup seasoned bread
  crumbs
½ cup Parmesan cheese
6 ounces cooked shrimp
6 ounces fresh lump
  crabmeat
1 teaspoon salt
1 teaspoon black pepper

Remove stems from the eggplants and split them oblong. Place eggplants in boiling water for 2 minutes, then put them in ice water. Scrape the meat from the eggplants and reserve skin. Sauté celery, onions, peppers and garlic in butter until soft. Mix with eggplant meat, olive oil, bread crumbs, Parmesan cheese, shrimp, crabmeat and seaonings; combine well. Put this stuffing back in the reserved skins and bake at 325 degrees for 20 minutes or until golden brown. Serves 4.

SCOTTO'S RISTORANTE ITALIANO'S
"RICHARD'S FAMOUS HOMEMADE CHEESECAKE"

Crust:

1 cup graham cracker crumbs

3 tablespoons melted butter
3 tablespoons sugar

Combine the ingredients and press into the bottom of a 9-inch springform pan.

1½ pounds cream cheese
¾ cup sugar
3 eggs

2 cups sour cream
1 teaspoon vanilla

When the cream cheese is at room temperature, combine it with the sugar in a mixer; cream the cheese with sugar until smooth. Add eggs one at a time, beating well after each addition. Add sour cream and vanilla. Pour the batter into a prepared crust and bake for 1 hour and 15 minutes at 300 degrees. Turn oven off and leave cheesecake in oven for 2 hours. Yields 1 cheesecake.

PERRY'S SEAFOOD HOUSE
Pensacola

PERRY'S SEAFOOD HOUSE

The old red house with the Perry's sign on its roof could tell many stories. The stories would begin in 1858, when the Caro family, who paved Pensacola's early streets with brick and ships' ballast, began construction of their two-story frame home. They would continue through the Civil War, when Pensacola was under siege.

The stories would go on to mention the lumber boom years of the 1880s when a watchman on the second floor searched for ships, then took a lantern and rowboat to pilot them through the sand-laden entrance to Bayou Chico. They would tell of the tollkeeper who ferried passengers across the channel. There would be stories of the well-known Gulf Coast artist, Manuel Runyan, who lived there and taught art on the front porch in the 1930s and 1940s. And undoubtedly there would be tales of the 1950s when it became a fraternity house for Pensacola Junior College.

For the last twenty years, ever since Perry Baniakis, Sr., opened his restaurant here, the house has been a familiar landmark to Pensacolans as *the* place to eat seafood. A wall of celebrity photos, ranging from June Allison and Bob Hope to John Wayne, Clint Eastwood and Pernell Roberts, shows it's not just sought out by locals, either.

Though a new gazebo-shaped bar with a pegged pine floor is "a little fancier," the main dining area at Perry's boasts a simple décor, with oak floors, the original fireplace and formica-topped tables. People come to Perry's not for the atmosphere, but for the good seafood—broiled, baked or fried. Gulf shrimp, scallops, Florida lobster, catfish and oysters are served with french fries or grits, cole slaw and hushpuppies.

According to Cliff Whitmore, son of the founder, Perry's was the first restaurant to serve scamp, now a popular fish. Scamp swims underneath snapper and used to be caught inadvertently. It became known as lady fish when fishermen started taking the fish to the red-light district to barter in the 1930s.

Perry's was also the first restaurant to serve snapper throats. Once, when snapper fillets were cut for shipping north, the throats were considered waste and were taken home by the workers to eat. But as soon as Perry's started serving them, the pure white, firm meat from the throat of the Pensacola red snapper became a culinary hit.

And judging from the ones I tasted, I can understand why. Served with Perry's own tartar and cocktail sauces, the freshly fried fish was delectable. Another favorite I sampled was their Key Lime Pie with a three-inch-high meringue. "When one of these pies is carried across the room," I was told, "every lady in the room starts ordering one."

I don't know about *every* lady, but I know this one did.— B.R.M.

Perry's Seafood House is located at 2140 South Barrancas Avenue in Pensacola. Hours are from 11:00 a.m. to 10:00 p.m. Sunday, Monday, Wednesday and Thursday, and until 11:00 p.m. on Friday and Saturday. The restaurant is closed Tuesday. Reservations are not accepted. For information call (904) 434-2995.

PERRY'S SEAFOOD HOUSE'S BAKED FISH

1 to 2 garlic cloves, crushed
1 cup olive oil
juice of 1 lemon

1 8- to 10-ounce grouper
fillet
parsley flakes for garnish

Mix garlic, olive oil and lemon juice. Rub the fish fillet with a little olive oil and bake at 350 to 400 degrees for 15 to 20 minutes or until done. When the fish is done, pour the garlic, olive oil and lemon mixture over it and sprinkle with parsley flakes. Serves 2.

PERRY'S SEAFOOD HOUSE'S REMOULADE SAUCE

3 cups chopped celery
1 bunch green onions
2 tablespoons dry mustard

½ gallon mayonnaise
6 anchovies, canned

Grind celery and onions into a paste in a meat grinder or food processor. Mix with other ingredients. This sauce is good on boiled shrimp served on a bed of lettuce. Yields approximately ¾ gallon.

PERRY'S SEAFOOD HOUSE'S COCKTAIL SAUCE

2 cups chili sauce
4 tablespoons Worcester-
shire sauce
2 cups ketchup
2 teaspoons dry mustard

2 teaspoons salt
4 tablespoons horseradish
(creamed)
3 teaspoons black pepper
juice of 1 lemon

Mix all the ingredients together and serve with oysters, scallops, shrimp or other boiled or fried seafood. Store in the refrigerator. Yields approximately 5 cups.

HOPKINS BOARDING HOUSE
Pensacola

HOPKINS BOARDING HOUSE

Diners from town, and from all over, sit elbow-to-elbow beside the boarders at Hopkins Boarding House in Pensacola. Perfect strangers are soon talking and laughing while mounds of home-cooked vegetables and meats and biscuits are passed around, family style. On Tuesday, Friday and Sunday, when the famous fried chicken is served, folks are lined up in droves.

Arkie "Ma" Hopkins opened her boarding house in 1948. The spacious two-story frame home, built in 1900, is located in the North Hills historic district and surrounded by wonderful old rambling houses and tree-filled yards.

Ma Hopkins ran a tight ship. No drinking was ever allowed on the premises, and no smoking and "no hats" were allowed at the table. When finished, everyone was expected to carry their plates to the kitchen. But her kindheartedness and gracious southern hospitality made the Hopkins Boarding House a Gulf Coast tradition. One boarder, now in his eighties, has liked it so much he's been there more than thirty years.

Since her death in December 1986, Mrs. Hopkins's son, Ed, an attorney, and her niece, Judy Viock, are continuing to run the boarding house in the same tradition. Ed Hopkins recalls childhood memories of his mother staying up all Saturday night cooking pies for Sunday dinner. Though they still serve cakes, cobblers and puddings, he told me, "Most people today generally have no room left for dessert."

The morning I visited, I was welcomed into the homey, oak-paneled, high-ceilinged dining room by Winnie Smith, who was raised by her older sister, Ma Hopkins. She had just finished snapping green beans for lunch.

In addition to twelve bushels of green beans a week, they serve a vast array of other fresh vegetables—like turnip greens, collards, pole beans, cabbage, carrots, butter beans, squash, okra and black-eyed peas—along with rice, gravy and muffins. Chicken and dumplings, beef stew, roast beef, ham, liver and fried chicken are served on alternating days.

After a tour of the house, I enjoyed a hearty breakfast of an omelet with grits, sausage and biscuits while I chatted with a few lingering customers. As I left I looked longingly at the front porch where "there's always a breeze" and wished I had time to do what so many diners do—just sit and rock a spell.—B.R.M.

Hopkins Boarding House is located at 900 North Spring Street in Pensacola. Breakfast hours are from 6:30 to 9:00 a.m.; lunch hours are from 11:15 to 2:00 p.m.; and dinner hours are from 5:15 to 7:00 p.m. The dining room is closed Sunday evening and all day Monday. For reservations call (904) 438-3979.

HOPKINS BOARDING HOUSE'S
STEWED OKRA AND TOMATOES

2 pounds fresh okra (or
  3 10-ounce packages
  frozen okra)
3 16-ounce cans tomatoes,
  chopped

1 cup chopped onions
¼ cup bacon drippings
salt and pepper to taste

Wash, trim and slice the okra. Combine all the ingredients. Do not sauté. Simmer on top of stove in a covered saucepan or skillet, or bake in a 350-degree oven in a tightly covered casserole for 30 to 45 minutes. Check okra for desired tenderness. Serves 8 to 10.

HOPKINS BOARDING HOUSE'S
SWEET POTATO SOUFFLE

4 cups mashed sweet
  potatoes
½ cup sugar
1 stick butter or margarine
½ cup grated coconut

⅓ cup raisins
1 teaspoon lemon extract (or
  orange peel)
1½ cups miniature
  marshmallows

While the potatoes are hot, add all the other ingredients except marshmallows. (If potatoes are dry, add up to ½ cup evaporated milk.) Place in a casserole dish and cover with marshmallows. Bake in a 300-degree oven until the marshmallows are brown, about 20 to 30 minutes. Serves 6.

11

HOPKINS BOARDING HOUSE'S
CHICKEN AND NOODLES

1 stewing chicken
3 quarts water
8 ounces flat egg noodles
2 cups tomato sauce
1 cup tomato paste

2 onions, chopped
1 green pepper, chopped
½ cup chopped celery
2 teaspoons oregano
salt and pepper to taste

Place chicken in a large pot and cover with water. Simmer until tender, an hour or so. Remove chicken from broth and let cool. Set aside. Cook noodles in the broth until almost tender. Add remaining ingredients; cover and simmer until vegetables are tender, about 30 minutes or so. While the vegetables are cooking, remove bones from the chicken and cut the meat into bite-size pieces. Return chicken pieces to the pot just before vegetables are done. Heat through and serve. Serves 6.

JAMIE'S FRENCH RESTAURANT
Pensacola

JAMIE'S FRENCH RESTAURANT

In a Victorian cottage in Pensacola a former schoolteacher is now educating an appreciative clientele on the wonders of fine French cooking.

Elizabeth Dasher, a Georgia native who gave up her place at the head of a classroom to study at the famed Culinary Institute of America in New York, is the chef at Jamie's French Restaurant. Since 1982 she and co-owner Gary Serafin have been pleasing the palates of local residents and visitors alike.

Jamie's is located in the Seville Historic District, an area of gracefully restored eighteenth- and nineteenth-century buildings on the bayfront. Nearby is the West Florida Museum of History and the Pensacola Historical Museum.

The four-room "shotgun-style" frame structure, with its tin roof and center hall, boasts a front porch complete with a swing. According to the owners, when the house was built in 1860 it was the practice to tax front-yard space; consequently the lot is small in the front and narrow and deep in the rear. Double fireplaces are still the only source of heat in the restaurant. Lace curtains, wallpaper decorated with birds and flowers in tones of burgundy and cream, wooden floors, pink linen tablecloths and fresh flowers provide a restful, lovely setting for the wonderfully prepared food.

Jamie's serves classic French cuisine. All the ingredients are guaranteed to be fresh, promises Gary Serafin. Their backyard herb garden provides many of the seasonings used.

Their specials vary daily, and the menu is changed every three months. Appetizers range from Stuffed Quail and Escargots Bourguignonne to Shrimp with Remoulade Sauce and Fettucine Alfredo with Pesto. Dinner entrées include Medallions of Beef with Morel Sauce, Veal Sweetbreads, chicken breast with a Grand Marnier and pecan sauce, and lamb chops.

I sampled two selections from the luncheon menu. The *potage du jour* was a delightful Cold Avocado Soup, smooth as silk with a tantalizing touch of lemon. The Croque Madam, made of a chicken breast, Swiss cheese and champagne mustard on sourdough bread, had been dipped in egg and sherry

14

and then sautéed, creating an unusual and delicious sandwich.

Looking around the room as I relished my own meal, I observed two businessmen engaged in serious conversation at one end of the room. At another table sat a grandmother, mother and a little girl dressed in ruffles and bows who was using her most lady-like manners. All were enjoying the fine food and ambiance of this genteel Victorian setting.—B.R.M.

Jamie's French Restaurant is located at 424 East Zaragosa Street in Pensacola. Lunch hours are 11:30 a.m. to 2:30 p.m. Tuesday through Saturday. Dinner hours are 6:00 to 10:00 p.m. Monday through Saturday. For reservations (recommended) call (904) 434-2911.

JAMIE'S FRENCH RESTAURANT'S SUPREME DE VOILAILLE MADAGASCAR

2 boneless chicken breasts
flour for dredging
2 ounces clarified butter
¼ cup chopped scallions
1 teaspoon crushed garlic

2 teaspoons crushed green
peppercorns
2 ounces Pernod
1 cup chicken stock
1 cup heavy cream

Slightly flatten the chicken breasts at the thick end with a mallet. Dredge chicken breasts in flour. Sauté over high heat in clarified butter. Remove chicken to a platter and keep it warm. Pour off butter from the skillet used to cook chicken. Return skillet to high heat. Add scallions, garlic and peppercorns and sauté for 30 seconds. Add Pernod and ignite the liquid. When flame reduces, add stock and reduce liquid to 3 tablespoons. Add heavy cream and reduce until sauce becomes thick. Pour sauce over chicken breasts and serve. Serves 2.

JAMIE'S FRENCH RESTAURANT'S ROASTED
RED PEPPER AND SAFFRON SAUCE

1 red bell pepper
pinch of saffron
1 teaspoon crushed
   tomatoes
1 teaspoon minced onions
1 teaspoon minced garlic

½ cup white wine
½ cup clam juice
1 cup heavy cream
pinch of thyme
1 teaspoon freshly chopped
   parsley

Roast the red pepper; peel and purée. In a saucepan, combine puréed pepper, saffron, tomatoes, onions, garlic, wine and clam juice. Reduce liquid to ¼ cup. Add heavy cream and reduce until mixture thickens and measures about ¾ cup. Remove sauce from heat. Add thyme and chopped parsley. This sauce can be used with most fish; just spoon over fish and serve. Serves 2.

JAMIE'S FRENCH RESTAURANT'S
COLD AVOCADO SOUP

4 cups avocado pulp
2 small tomatoes, peeled,
   seeded and finely
   chopped
¼ cup minced onion
2 teaspoons minced garlic
¼ cup mayonnaise
1½ cups chicken stock

2 tablespoons lemon or
   lime juice
2½ cups heavy cream
salt and pepper to taste
dash of cayenne
lemon or lime peel for
   garnish

Blend the above ingredients until well incorporated and chill for 4 to 6 hours. Serve in bowls or cups and top with a twist of lemon or lime peel. Serves 8.

1912 THE RESTAURANT
Pensacola

1912 THE RESTAURANT The first time I saw the Pensacola Hilton was by accident. A few years ago, I was traveling with my family to Alabama, and we took a foray into Pensacola to see the Seville Historic District. "Stop!" I yelled, "I want to see that restored train station."

The lobby, with the original hexagonal mosaic tile and ticket windows, was breathtaking. "Good for the Hilton," I said, "and hooray for preservation!"

On my latest trip there, it was a pleasure to see the hotel bustling with conference delegates, enjoying the charm of the past enhanced with modern amenities.

Listed on the National Register of Historic Places, the L & N passenger depot was built of yellow brick in 1912—1913 at a cost of $150,000. It served the Pensacola rail industry for fifty-eight years, until 1971 when the last train rolled out. After years of disrepair, the depot was purchased by developers who spent $2 million on the restoration as part of the Hilton Hotel project, completed in June 1984. The French clay-tile roof was removed piece by piece, coded, cleaned and reinstalled. The ceramic tile floors, the marble baseboards and the oak stair rails and window casings throughout the building were returned to their original rich luster. A fifteen-story glass addition tucked between the depot and the railroad tracks houses the hotel rooms.

1912 the Restaurant is located in a room added to the terminal in the 1930s to handle baggage storage. Its handsome interior, done in shades of mauve and teal, is highlighted by brass inlaid mirrors from the first building of Lloyd's of London.

Seafood is offered in abundance, as are steak and prime rib, with many dishes prepared tableside. I sampled an interesting appetizer of baked Brie with pecans, served with grapes and slices of poppyseed bread. A tasty sea-and-citrus salad combined crabmeat and shrimp with orange and grapefruit segments.

On Friday and Saturday nights, live entertainment is featured. The restaurant also offers a fabulous Sunday brunch.

This is the sort of place you want to dress up for; in fact a coat and tie are requested at lunch and required at dinner.— B.R.M.

1912 the Restaurant is located in the Pensacola Hilton at 200 East Gregory Street in Pensacola. Lunch is served from 11:00 a.m. to 2:00 p.m. Monday through Friday. Sunday brunch is served from 10:00 a.m. to 2:00 p.m. Dinner is served daily from 6:00 p.m. to 10:00 p.m. For reservations call (904) 433-3336.

1912 THE RESTAURANT'S SCALLOPS SAUTE

1 tablespoon clarified butter
¼ teaspoon minced garlic
1 teaspoon minced shallots
6 ounces scallops
½ teaspoon dill
⅓ cup sliced mushrooms
½ lemon
⅛ cup white wine
¼ teaspoon parsley
4 butter pats (about 2 tablespoons)

Coat a sauté pan with clarified butter. Heat the butter and add garlic and shallots. Add scallops and sauté until almost done. Remove scallops. Add dill, mushrooms, a squeeze of lemon and the white wine. Let the sauce reduce. Add scallops again and stir. Add parsley and mix. Remove from heat and add pats of butter. Serves 1.

1912 THE RESTAURANT'S L & N NEPTUNE

1 8-ounce New York strip
  steak
1 slice toasted bread
2 ounces crabmeat

2 large prawns
1 tablespoon butter
3 tablespoons Béarnaise
  Sauce (see Index)

Cook steak to order. Place it on a slice of toasted bread on a warm plate. Sauté crabmeat and prawns in butter for 3 minutes or so and place on top of the steak. Top with Béarnaise Sauce. Serves 1.

THE GOLDEN PHEASANT
Tallahassee

THE GOLDEN PHEASANT Within easy lobbying distance of Florida's state capitol is the Governor's Inn and its elegant restaurant, the Golden Pheasant. Located on a brick-paved street in Tallahassee's downtown historic district, the small hotel caters to those who appreciate personal service and well-bred civility with their lodgings.

The inn and restaurant are owned by Lawton M. Chiles III, son of Flordia's senior United States senator, and his wife Kitty. They created the hotel by combining two buildings constructed in the 1930s as retail stores selling hardware, office supplies and gifts. Each of the forty-one rooms—handsomely furnished with antiques and reproductions—is named for a deceased governor of Florida.

The Golden Pheasant, now attached to the Governor's Inn, is in a yellow brick building constructed in the early 1930s to house Bennett's College Inn Pharmacy and Bennett's Beauty Shop.

The restaurant is discreetly luxurious. The main dining room, decorated in tones of rose and seafoam, is wallpapered in silk moire, accented with a reproduction of an early nineteenth-century French mural. Lace and linen curtains, polished silver and Empire chairs with soft down cushions create an atmosphere of comfort and dignity.

High standards have been set for their cuisine as well. Manager David Ferguson told me that absolutely nothing is made ahead of time; all food is fresh and cooked to order. The kitchen does not have a microwave, not even a can opener. Chef Bill Narhi, a protégé of John Shoop, who is now an instructor at the Culinary Institute in New York, creates excitingly different dishes, whether using fresh grouper from Florida or fresh lion from Africa.

The evening I dined at the Golden Pheasant was filled with one pleasure after another. An appetizer of Seafood Mousseline with Mushroom Cream Sauce was a work of art; the soup, Chilled Tomato-Basil Soup with Champagne, was wonderful. A refreshing sorbet followed, to awaken the palate for the pièce de résistance—Roast Partridge with Veal Mousse and Sauce Madeira, served with snow peas and tiny potatoes. It was superb, though a taste of my generous dinner companion's entrée, Duckling Lapérouse with Muscatel Wine Sauce, left me in doubt as to which of us had made the better selection.

The leisurely, beautifully served meal was brought to a conclusion with homemade Coffee Ice Cream and Marjolaine, a multilayered feat of chocolate, hazelnuts, praline and cream, mastered, I was told, by only twelve chefs in the country. It was an altogether unforgettable dinner.—B.R.M.

The Golden Pheasant is located in the Governor's Inn at 109 East College Avenue in Tallahassee. Lunch is served from 11:30 a.m. to 2:00 p.m. Monday through Friday. Dinner is served from 6:00 p.m. to 10:00 p.m. Monday through Saturday. The restaurant is closed Sunday. Reservations are recommended; phone (904) 222-0241.

THE GOLDEN PHEASANT'S DUCKLING LAPEROUSE WITH MUSCATEL WINE SAUCE

½ ounce oil
1 breast of duck
2 teaspoons Dijon mustard
2 ounces grated Gruyère or
  Swiss cheese

1 ounce raspings (toasted
  bread crumbs)

Heat oil in a skillet until it smokes; add duck, skin side down. As the fat cooks out of the duck skin, keep pouring fat out of the skillet. As the fat is being cooked out, gradually reduce the heat. The end product should be a very crisp duck skin with very little of the breast meat having been cooked. Remove duck from the skillet and place on a towel, skin side down. Allow it to cool.

When the breast is cool, brush Dijon mustard over the entire skin and then top with cheese. Lastly, sprinkle raspings on top. To finish cooking the duck for service, put it on an ovenproof plate, skin side up. Place in a preheated oven set at 400 degrees for approximately 10 minutes. Duck should be pink and juicy inside. Slice into thin slices and serve with sauce. Serves 1.

23

Sauce:

½ cup Muscatel Wine
2 ounces game or chicken stock
1 sage leaf
1 shallot, chopped

½ cup demi-glace or plain
brown gravy
salt and pepper to taste

Pour fat off the same skillet and return to heat. Pour wine into the hot skillet and scrape all the drippings off the bottom, using a wooden spoon. Add stock, sage and shallots to skillet. Reduce to about 3 ounces and add the demi-glace or gravy. Season to taste. Cook on low heat about 5 minutes. Strain sauce through a fine wire strainer and pour onto cooked, sliced duck.

THE GOLDEN PHEASANT'S CREME CARAMEL

Caramel:

1 cup sugar

Put sugar in a 10-inch skillet set over high heat; stir often. When sugar is almost completely melted, lower heat and stir until caramel is free of all lumps and is a deep amber color. Immediately pour into 4 8-ounce ramekins so the caramel just covers the bottom. Set aside and continue with recipe.

¾ cup sugar
4 eggs
2 egg yolks
2 cups milk
1 2-inch section of vanilla
   bean (or 1 teaspoon
   vanilla extract)

1 cup whipped cream
1 tablespoon toasted
   almonds

Thoroughly whisk sugar into eggs and yolks. Place milk and split vanilla bean in a double boiler and heat until almost boiling. Whisk hot milk into egg-sugar mixture. Strain through a fine mesh strainer and pour into prepared ramekins. Place ramekins in a roasting pan. Fill with water up to the halfway mark of the ramekins; cover with foil and bake in a preheated, 225-degree oven for 1½ to 2 hours until custard is set. Remove from oven and cool. At serving time, run a sharp knife around the edge of the ramekins to loosen caramel. Unmold on a plate and serve with whipped cream and toasted almonds. Serves 4.

WAKULLA SPRINGS LODGE
Wakulla Springs

WAKULLA SPRINGS LODGE **I** am torn. Part of me wants to let you know about this "nature lover's paradise," where you really can get away from it all, and the other part wants to keep it a secret. The springs here are so ancient that the same mastodon bones seen by Ponce de Leon in 1513 can still be seen at the bottom of the one-hundred-and-eighty-five-foot, crystal-clear springs. The Indians called the place Wakulla, "mysteries of strange waters." Ponce de Leon believed it was the fountain of youth. When neither he nor his crew grew any younger, Ponce de Leon left, disillusioned. Six years later, feeling that he had been hasty, he returned to the springs but found hostile Indians. They fought in a battle that subsequently resulted in the explorer's death.

Soon after entering the 1937 lodge built by Edward Ball, I realized that this was a place to relax and take off your watch. The lobby is dominated by a great stone fireplace, and its cypress ceiling is decorated with murals hand-painted by a German craftsman believed to have once served Kaiser Wilhelm. Crossing the rose-and-beige marble floors I went to my room, which had spindle beds, its original Persian rug and a great view of the dock.

Within minutes I was at that dock preparing to board their jungle cruise. Live alligators swam beside us, and we photographed hundreds of unusual birds and other wildlife before switching to a glass-bottomed boat. This boat allowed us to watch tropical fish thread through the natural underwater cliffs in this crystal-clear spring, which flows at an incredible rate of six hundred thousand gallons a minute.

The cruise certainly worked up my appetite, so I headed straight for the dining room upon docking. It's hard to put a name to the dining room's décor. The green, flowered tablecloths, old-fashioned rose-patterned china and black-leather rocking chairs make you think of a more comfortable time. The cuisine itself conjured up a southern plantation which belied the décor. I ordered their Cornish Game Hen, very tender and moist with a yummy stuffing. My collaborator,

26

Becky, told me not to leave without getting their Blueberry Sour Cream Pie, so I sampled both that and the Key Lime Pie. The Key Lime was delicious, and the marriage of tartish blueberries with sour cream and whipped cream was an ideal union.

For any getaway, this lodge and four-thousand-acre wildlife sanctuary offer a one-of-a-kind experience that I suppose I shouldn't keep to myself.

Wakulla Springs Lodge is located fifteen miles south of Tallahassee on Highway 61 South. Breakfast is served from 7:30 a.m. until 10:00 a.m.; lunch from noon until 2:00 p.m.; and dinner from 6:30 p.m. until 8:30 p.m., daily. For reservations, call (904) 224-5950.

WAKULLA SPRINGS LODGE'S BLUEBERRY SOUR CREAM PIE

1 cup sugar
½ teaspoon salt
¼ cup all-purpose flour
2 eggs
2 cups sour cream

¾ teaspoon vanilla
1 9-inch graham cracker pie shell, unbaked
1 can blueberry pie filling
1 cup whipped cream

In a mixing bowl combine the first 6 ingredients and mix well. Pour into the pie shell and bake in a preheated, 350-degree oven for 30 minutes or until the center is set. Top hot pie with blueberry filling. Chill several hours. When ready to serve, top with whipped cream. Yields 1 pie.

WAKULLA SPRINGS LODGE'S STUFFED CORNISH HENS SUPREME WITH WILD RICE

4 1½-pound Cornish hens
1¼ cups chopped scallions
1 cup chopped mushrooms
2 tablespoons butter
2 cups soft bread crumbs
1 hard-boiled egg, chopped
¼ cup sour cream
¼ teaspoon garlic salt

⅛ teaspoon pepper
¾ cup milk
½ cup water
1 envelope chicken gravy mix (commercial)
2 dashes of ground nutmeg
1 4-ounce package wild rice, cooked

27

Rinse hens and pat them dry. Cook 1 cup of the onions and ½ cup of the mushrooms in butter until tender and the liquid evaporates. Combine with bread crumbs, egg, sour cream, garlic salt and pepper. Lightly stuff hens with this mixture; truss. Place hens, breast side up, in a large, shallow baking pan. Cover with foil and roast in a 350-degree oven for 1 hour. Uncover; baste with drippings, spoon off and save 2 tablespoons of drippings. Return hens to oven and roast 30 to 40 minutes or until tender and browned. Sauté remaining onions and mushrooms in reserved drippings in a small saucepan. Stir in milk, water, gravy mix and nutmeg; bring to a boil, stirring. Simmer 1 minute. Serve hens with this sauce on a bed of wild rice. Serves 4.

WAKULLA SPRINGS LODGE'S NAVY BEAN SOUP

1 pound dried navy beans
5 cups water
1 10-ounce can beef
  consommé
1 chicken bouillon cube
4 potatoes, diced

2 onions, diced
4 tablespoons butter
4 carrots, diced
2 cups chopped ham
3 bay leaves
salt and pepper to taste

Soak beans overnight in enough water to cover them. Rinse and place navy beans, water, consommé and bouillon cube in a large pot. Bring to a boil; then cover and simmer for 2 hours. Add potatoes to soup pot. Sauté onions in butter until partially cooked. Add to soup pot along with remaining ingredients. Simmer, covered, for 1 hour or until vegetables are done. Serves 6 to 8.

1878 STEAK HOUSE
Fernandina Beach

1878 STEAK HOUSE   One of Florida's most beautiful restaurants is the product of the transformation of an 1878 warehouse into a steak house with a Victorian décor. Its story really began back in 1852 when C. H. Huot came to Fernandina from France. At that time Fernandina's natural deep-water harbor attracted cargo ships from around the world. But in 1862, when twenty-six ships full of Federal troops came to seize the port, local citizens chose to set the business district on fire rather than surrender it. Then in 1877 disaster struck again when yellow fever afflicted a thousand people out of a total population of sixteen hundred.

Huot watched those bleak times come and go. In 1878, with the continued expansion of the railroad and of port activity, he felt the harbor needed a sturdy warehouse. Soon his building was not only storing materials, it was also functioning as a gathering place for local merchants and seamen. Here the sailors swapped news of their crossings while merchants inspected bins of coffee and tea or the lumber that was harvested in northern Florida and hauled here by ox-drawn wagons.

After an age of prosperity, Fernandina again drifted into a decline. Not until a revival in tourism was the city spurred into the renovation of its quaint historic harbor district. In 1974 Gene Oviatt decided the neglected warehouse would make a fine steak house, and he set about to refurbish it.

The night that I wound my way through potted trees up the stairway to the elegant blue-and-rose dining room, I couldn't believe that I was in Florida. This was the first restaurant I visited in the state, and I had never really thought of the Victorian era or its décor in conjunction with the Sunshine State. But here it was—antique sideboards, paisley wallpaper and bentwood chairs.

Sitting beside a black fireplace, I watched as the chef cooked my Beef Forestière in their open grill. While watching the preparation, I enjoyed their French Onion Soup, which had a rich, velvety-thick consistency, and a little salad with a heavenly dressing, the recipe for which I couldn't pry out of the chef. The restaurant is known for its beef, which is superb, but don't forsake their other dishes. Pompano Toulouse is quite good, and the Russian Crème dessert with Melba sauce reminded me of the décor itself—sumptuous and rich!

The 1878 Steak House is located at 12 North Second Street in Fernandina Beach. Lunch is served from 11:30 a.m. until 2:00 p.m. Monday through Friday from May through September. Dinner is served daily from 5:00 p.m. until 10:00 p.m. from May through October; it is served Monday through Saturday other months. Reservations are not accepted, but for further information call (904) 261-4049.

1878 STEAK HOUSE'S BEEF FORESTIERE

1 6- to 8-ounce center-cut
   rib-eye
5 to 6 shallots, chopped
   fine
3 tablespoons butter
½ cup chopped mushrooms
2 pinches of cracked black
   pepper

6 ounces Brown Sauce
   (recipe below)
3 teaspoons Dijon mustard
½ ounce dry vermouth
½ ounce Madeira

Broil rib-eye and reserve the natural juices. Set steak aside. Sauté shallots in butter until pale. Add mushrooms and cracked pepper. Stir in Brown Sauce. Add au jus from broiled steak, mustard, vermouth and Madeira and stir until the mixture reaches a fast boil, but do not let it thicken. Pour over broiled rib-eye. Serves 1.

Brown Sauce:
2 tablespoons butter
¼ cup all-purpose flour
4 cups beef stock or broth
1 cup chopped tomatoes
1 medium carrot, coarsely
   grated
1 medium onion, coarsely
   grated

1 stalk celery, finely
   chopped
pinch of thyme
1 bay leaf, crushed
2 tablespoons sherry

31

In a saucepan melt butter and add flour, stirring into a paste. Stir over low heat until mixture browns. Gradually add stock, stirring constantly. Add all the remaining ingredients. Simmer until sauce is reduced by half. Strain through a sieve before serving. Leftover sauce can be frozen for other uses. Yields approximately 3 cups.

1878 STEAK HOUSE'S RUSSIAN CREME

1¾ cups heavy cream   1½ cups sour cream
10 tablespoons sugar   ¾ teaspoon vanilla
1 tablespoon gelatin

Place heavy cream and sugar in a saucepan and stir until it combines. Add gelatin and stir constantly over low heat until mixture reaches 120 degrees; remove from heat. In a stainless steel bowl combine sour cream and vanilla until well mixed. Whip sour cream mixture into the heavy cream mixture until thoroughly incorporated. Pour into 2½-ounce molds and cover with plastic wrap. Refrigerate for 24 hours. Serve with Melba Sauce. Serves 9.

Melba Sauce:
4 cups strawberries, sliced   1½ ounces triple sec
1½ ounces vodka   honey and sugar to taste
1½ ounces dark rum

Stir all the ingredients together and cool in the refrigerator for at least 1 hour before serving.

THE PALACE SALOON
Fernandina Beach

THE PALACE SALOON

I am told that people come to the Palace Saloon just to drink in the atmosphere, if nothing else. The heavy, red velvet draperies admit a bare slice of sunlight, giving the room a feeling of intimacy. Patrons will appreciate the hand-carved black mahogany caryatids supporting the mirror over the forty-foot bar, and the old, polished oak tables and mosaic tile floor. When you come to the Palace Saloon, you feel as if you'd stepped into a very fancy saloon in an old western movie.

In 1878 Josiah H. Prescott, who served as a Union lieutenant during the occupation of Fernandina in the Civil War, returned here to begin his haberdashery and shoe business. Before erecting his Renaissance Revival building, Prescott anchored the foundation in six feet of crushed oyster shells. It was not until 1903 that German-born Louis G. Hirth turned the structure into a saloon. Old advertisements reveal that the saloon offered Red Cross Rye, Turkey Mountain Corn Whiskey and Cognac Bouchée Frères. Hirth was obviously of a literary bent, for in 1907 he hired Roy Kennard to paint the literary murals that still hang above the marble wainscotting.

Back in those days, before ladies frequented saloons, the story goes that a local woman was showing a visiting friend around town one day on horseback. Her daring friend wanted to see the inside of the Palace Saloon, so she and her hostess rode their horses right through the swinging doors and up to the bar. The bartender, not to be outdone, promptly poured a beer for the horse, which the thirsty animal reportedly drank in one gulp!

For a short while during Prohibition, the saloon served as an ice-cream parlor, but it has continued as a bar ever since, and it now serves lunch.

The first thing I learned while touring the premises is that this is the kind of place where you can't remain a stranger for very long. The regulars insisted that I try the infamous twenty-two-ounce House Punch. I'm not sure what was in this pungent fruit-based drink except rum and gin, but I do know that more than one is bound to end your work day. I ordered

34

their Tuna Salad and learned the ingredient that made it so exceptional was simply fresh tuna. The regulars insisted that I sample bites of their lunches too. The Chicken Salad features crunchy almonds and sweet white grapes. They were sold out of their Seafood Salad, but the regulars vouched for its tastiness as well.

The Palace Saloon is the kind of place where even strangers feel at ease, where life's pressures seem to melt away. "Relaxation" isn't listed on the menu, but you can almost always find it here.

The Palace Saloon is located at 117 Centre Street in Fernandina Beach. Lunch is served from 11:30 a.m. to 3:00 p.m. daily. The bar is open from 8:30 a.m. to 1:00 a.m. Monday through Thursday, and until 2:00 a.m. on Friday and Saturday. Reservations aren't necessary, but for additional information call (904) 261-9068.

THE PALACE SALOON'S TUNA SALAD

1 pound fresh tuna (or 1 14-ounce can)
½ cup pickle relish, drained
½ stalk celery, chopped fine

4 hard-boiled eggs
juice of 1 lemon
salt and pepper to taste
½ cup mayonnaise

Coarsely chop the tuna. (Drain if using canned tuna.) Place tuna in a mixing bowl and add pickle relish and celery. Peel and chop eggs and add them to mixture. Add lemon juice, salt, pepper and mayonnaise. Mix until all ingredients are well combined and seasoned. Cover and refrigerate. Serves 8.

THE PALACE SALOON'S CHICKEN SALAD

2½ pounds chicken,
  cooked and diced
¾ pound white seedless
  grapes
½ stalk celery, chopped
  fine

1½ cups thinly sliced
  almonds
1 teaspoon Accent
1 teaspoon salt
1 cup mayonnaise

Place diced chicken in a large mixing bowl. Cut grapes into quarters and add them. Toss in the celery and add almonds; then add Accent and salt. Add mayonnaise, less or more as desired, thoroughly mixing to combine all ingredients and seasonings. Cover and refrigerate. Serves 12.

LE PAVILLON
St. Augustine

LE PAVILLON

The owners of Le Pavillon were somewhat taken aback when the chauffeur-driven limousine pulled up one day and an armed bodyguard came in to check the place out, followed by actress Brooke Shields and her mother, who had come for lunch. Like numerous other celebrities, they had made a special trip to St. Augustine to taste the culinary wonders of Le Pavillon.

Since 1977, when chef Claude Sinatsch and his German-born wife Giselle opened their restaurant in a charming old home on San Marco Avenue, Le Pavillon has won a wide reputation for its continental cuisine. Small wonder, since Claude was trained in Switzerland at the hotel his family owned, the Sports Hotel in Davos. He later worked as a chef at internationally renowned hotels in Europe and Bermuda before deciding to join his brother-in-law in St. Augustine.

"We always liked Florida," he told me, "and we fell in love with the European style of St. Augustine."

The family lives in the upstairs of the spacious house they purchased for Le Pavillon. The original structure was built before the turn of the century as a five-room cottage. Located in the Abbott Tract along what was once Route 1, it was a popular tourist home for many years, with vacationers returning season after season. Additions were built by every new owner, including the Sinatsches, who added a room in front to enlarge their seating area.

The interior of the restaurant, decorated by Giselle, is warm and mellow, with stained glass, lace curtains, a wooden mantel and fireplace, and antique glassware in curio cabinets. The bar is framed by the beautifully carved pineapple posts of a century-old bed.

Everyone in the family works at the restaurant. Claude cooks, Giselle works "up front," her brother, Fritz Dold, is the maître d', daughter Patricia serves and teen-aged son Claude helps "when he's not out surfing."

The night I was there it was raining outside, and the Sinatsches made me feel very much like I was a guest in their cozy home.

Le Pavillon is well known for its crêpes and veal. "And some say our rack of lamb is the best in the country," volunteered Giselle. Seasonal specialties such as quail, venison and goulash are also offered. But nothing could have been better than the bouillabaise they served me. Succulent pieces of fresh seafood, perfectly seasoned, exquisitely presented and accompanied by freshly made rolls with herb butter and a glass of excellent German wine—pure bliss!—B.R.M.

Le Pavillon is located at 45 San Marco Avenue in St. Augustine. Lunch hours are from 11:30 a.m. to 2:30 p.m.; dinner hours are from 5:00 to 10:00 p.m. every day. Reservations are recommended for weekends. Call (904) 824-6202.

LE PAVILLON'S POULET AU FROMAGE

1 8-ounce boneless chicken breast
1 mushroom, diced
1 small shallot, diced
1½ tablespoons sherry wine
¼ teaspoon freshly chopped parsley
salt to taste
freshly ground pepper to taste
2 thin slices Swiss cheese
2 pats butter
2 thin slices mozzarella cheese
breading
oil for deep-frying

Flatten the chicken breast with a mallet and set it aside. Sauté mushrooms and shallots for several minutes and then add sherry and parsley. Cook until most of the liquid has evaporated, and remove from heat. Lay out flattened breast and season with salt and pepper. Top with the Swiss cheese, the mushroom mixture, the butter pats and finally the mozzarella. Fold the breast in half. Bread the chicken and deep-fry it in oil; then bake it in the oven at 450 degrees for 10 to 15 minutes. (Or flour it and sauté in butter until lightly browned, and poach in stock with a dash of sherry until done.) You may serve with a poulette, supreme or Madeira sauce. Serves 1.

LE PAVILLON'S CLAUDE'S BOUILLABAISE

2 pounds seafood (lobster,
fresh mussels, clams,
haddock, turbot or brill,
whiting, eel and
crabmeat)
2 large onions, chopped
3 cloves garlic, crushed
2 tomatoes, chopped
½ cup oil
sprig of thyme, chopped

sprig of fennel, chopped
bay leaf
pinch of fresh saffron
salt and pepper to taste
strip of orange peel
4 cups boiling water
4 to 6 slices French bread
sprig of parsley, chopped
4 to 6 pats herbed butter

Cut the fish into 2-inch lengths, keeping the coarse and the more delicate fish on separate plates. Put the chopped onions, garlic and tomatoes in a saucepan with the oil, herbs, seasonings and orange peel. Add the coarser varieties of fish, cover with boiling water and cook for 5 minutes on a very quick fire. Then put in the remaining fish and continue boiling fish for another 5 minutes (10 minutes hard boiling altogether). Remove from heat. Strain the liquid into soup plates on slices of French bread. Arrange fish on top; sprinkle with chopped parsley. Top with a dab of herbed butter. Serves 4 to 6.

NOTE: The object of this very fast boiling is to blend the oil and water thoroughly. In slower cooking, the oil would not mix properly and would rise to the surface. And if the fish is cooked any longer, it will break and spoil in appearance and flavor.

SANTA MARIA
St. Augustine

SANTA MARIA

For years, throngs of hungry customers have flocked to the Santa Maria restaurant on the pier in St. Augustine to enjoy eating the seafood on their plates—and to enjoy feeding the fish in the water below.

Ever since the 1950s when the present owner's father, Louis S. Connell, started feeding fish daily from his restaurant, thousands of mullet, catfish, trout and sea bass have begged for their supper. As the fish jump and splash, the human diners watch and open trapdoors at their tables to oblige the fish with tidbits.

The Santa Maria is as nautical an atmosphere as you could want. Not only is the restaurant surrounded by water, with beautiful views of moored sailboats, but the décor itself features fishnets and ropes and ships' lanterns and wheels.

In 1763, shortly before Spain lost Florida to Great Britain, Spaniards built the first pier on Matanzas Bay on the site where the Santa Maria stands today. In the 1860s, Civil War soldiers enjoyed the pier while recuperating at an adjacent hospital. Following a fire in 1885, the pier was rebuilt, complete with a building that served as a house, then a fish market and, finally, following World War II as a restaurant.

Hurricane Dora tore up much of the eastern side of the restaurant in 1964, though as much as possible of the original structure was saved. Current owners Carl and Sylvia Connell proudly showed me the 1885 slatted wood ceiling in the bar, the original three-inch-thick heart-pine floors and their collection of historic photographs.

The Connells are always expanding, it seems, to make room for the crowds that frequent the restaurant during "the season" from February, when the Daytona 500 is held, through Labor Day. "We've done a project a year," Sylvia told me. "We're adding a porch now."

Though steak, chicken and spaghetti are served for die-hard landlubbers, the Santa Maria specializes in broiled flounder and a seafood platter with fried shrimp, oysters, deviled crab, scallops, clams and fish. A children's menu is also offered.

I couldn't resist sampling their satisfying Black Bean Soup, which the Connells often are asked to bring to community gatherings. The Shrimp Creole—made with Sylvia's own recipe—was spicy and wonderful. And oh, those Hushpuppies. They are uniquely sweet and good. The secret, Sylvia says, is to beat them well. "All that air beaten in makes them light."

The Santa Maria is very much a family-run restaurant with a friendly atmosphere in which people of all ages feel welcome. My only problem was what to leave to feed the fish.—B.R.M.

The Santa Maria is located on the pier at 135 Avenida Menendez in St. Augustine. Hours are from 11:30 a.m. to 11:00 p.m. every day except Tuesday and Wednesday, when the restaurant is open for dinner only, from 4:30 to 11:00 p.m. No reservations are accepted. For information call (904) 829-6578.

SANTA MARIA'S BLACK BEAN SOUP

1 12-ounce bag dry black beans	5 bay leaves
2 cloves garlic, chopped	½ cup cumin
1 medium onion, chopped fine	1 tablespoon thyme
1 medium bell pepper, chopped fine	½ cup red wine vinegar
½ cup olive oil	salt and pepper to taste
2 small ham hocks	6 to 8 cups cooked rice
	½ cup chopped scallions for garnish

Soak beans overnight. Do not drain. When you're ready to cook the beans, add more water, enough to measure 3 inches over top of the beans. Cook on medium-high heat. Sauté garlic, onions and bell peppers in olive oil; add to beans along with other ingredients, except vinegar, salt and pepper. Cook for about 2½ hours or until tender. Add vinegar, salt and pepper and cook another 30 minutes. Put 1 cup of the cooked beans in a blender and purée; add to beans and cook 15 more minutes, or until beans thicken. Serve over rice and top with scallions. Serves 8.

SANTA MARIA'S SHRIMP CREOLE

4 16-ounce cans tomatoes
1 large onion, coarsely chopped
1 large bell pepper, coarsely chopped
4 stalks celery, coarsely chopped
1 cup olive oil
6 bay leaves
2 cloves garlic, chopped
1 tablespoon thyme
1 tablespoon oregano
⅓ cup gumbo filé
salt and pepper to taste
¼ cup cornstarch
2 tablespoons water
1½ pounds fresh, medium shrimp, peeled and deveined
4 sticks butter (or margarine)
4 cups cooked rice

Cook tomatoes over medium heat. Meanwhile, in a sauté pan, sauté onions, bell peppers and celery in olive oil; add to tomatoes. Add all other ingredients, except cornstarch, butter, shrimp and rice. Cook 2 hours on medium heat. Add cornstarch to enough water to dissolve it, then pour into tomato mixture. Cook an additional 30 minutes, stirring occasionally. Sauté shrimp in butter until tender, then add both shrimp and butter to tomato mixture. Cook 5 more minutes. Serve over rice. Serves 8 to 10.

SANTA MARIA'S HUSHPUPPIES

2 cups self-rising flour
1 cup cornmeal
1 large onion, chopped fine
½ cup sugar
1 tablespoon salt
1 tablespoon pepper
½ to 1 cup water
deep-fat for frying

Mix the first 6 ingredients together. Add water, leaving mix thick enough to dip from a teaspoon. Beat well with an electric mixer, making sure to beat long enough to make the dough light and air-filled. Drop like dumplings into enough hot grease to cover them. Fry until brown. Serves 12.

RAINTREE RESTAURANT
St. Augustine

RAINTREE RESTAURANT

Like much earlier English settlers, the MacDonald family sailed across the Atlantic to America in hopes of realizing their dreams and ambitions in the New World. They sold most of their belongings and began their voyage on March 30, 1979, in a forty-five-foot yacht. They stopped at the Canaries, then Barbados, before reaching St. Augustine, which they had liked on an earlier visit.

Once settled in St. Augustine, the enterprising MacDonalds bought and renovated the Victorian house at 102 San Marco Avenue, turning it into a stunningly beautiful restaurant.

The house was built in 1879 by Bernard Masters, a Confederate veteran who provided houses for each of his five daughters. It became the residence of daughter Hattie after her marriage to A. J. Collins, who was in the dry goods business. After World War II, the house was converted into the Corner House restaurant, well known for its southern cooking.

The MacDonalds have added a glassed-in room to the front porch where musicians now entertain, and they have built a lovely, landscaped courtyard at the side entrance to the restaurant. The inside rooms have been decorated with exquisite wallpaper and authentic antiques. The 1650 Jacobean cradle and the 1415 chair in the hallway are family pieces of the MacDonalds.

As in many historic restaurants, the entire family is involved in running the business. Tristan MacDonald manages the restaurant. His wife, Alex, and daughter, Lorna, run the front; and his son Gaere, who has cooked since he was fourteen, is the chef.

Their goal is to give St. Augustine diners "fine food in beautiful surroundings." Their numerous culinary awards attest to their continuing success. Tristan pointed out the new temperature-controlled cases that display more than seven hundred bottles of wine. "*Wine Spectator* magazine rated us as having one of the two hundred and fifty outstanding wine lists in the world," he said with pride.

Raintree offers diners a wealth of options. Appetizers range from Truffle Pâté and escargots to homemade soups. Entrées include Veal Saltimbocca, Brandy Pepper Steak, Chicken Florentine and Filet Mignon Béarnaise. Seafood is especially well prepared here, from Bourbon Street Lobster and Rainbow Trout Amandine to Blackened Redfish.

"We have an outstanding dessert chef," Tristan told me. And from the looks of the pastry cart, I knew he was right. The sinfully rich Fudge Brownie Tart proved irresistible . . . and worth every calorie.—B.R.M.

Raintree Restaurant is located at 102 San Marco Avenue in St. Augustine. It is open for lunch on weekdays, from 11:30 a.m. to 2:30 p.m. Dinner is served daily from 5:00 to 9:30 p.m. Reservations are recommended and are necessary on weekends; call (904) 824-7211.

RAINTREE RESTAURANT'S FUDGE BROWNIE TART

1 stick butter
6 ounces semisweet
  chocolate
1½ cups sugar
3 eggs
½ cup chopped pecans

¾ cup flour
1 uncooked pastry tart shell
½ cup chopped pecans
8 ounces semisweet
  chocolate
1 cup heavy cream

Melt butter and 6 ounces of the chocolate in the top of a double boiler. Add sugar, eggs, pecans and flour; mix well. Pour into a pastry shell. Sprinkle chopped nuts around the edge of the brownie mix and bake at 350 degrees for 20 to 25 minutes.

Melt 8 ounces of chocolate with the cream; bring slowly to a boil and pour a thin layer of chocolate sauce in the center of the tart. Let remaining sauce cool along with the tart. When cool, remove tart and cut into 12 slices. Take cooled chocolate sauce and whip until smooth and of piping consistency. Pipe desired decoration on top of tart. Serves 12.

RAINTREE RESTAURANT'S SWORDFISH IN PINEAPPLE TARRAGON SAUCE

1 stick butter
1 medium onion, diced
1 pineapple, cored, peeled
  and diced
1 teaspoon tarragon
½ cup sherry
½ cup lobster stock (or clam
  broth)

½ cup whipping cream
salt and pepper to taste
6 8-ounce swordfish steaks
½ cup flour
splash of white wine

In a large saucepan, melt the butter. Steam the onions in the butter with the lid on, until the onions are soft and translucent. Add the pineapple and tarragon; cook for a further 2 minutes to allow the herb flavor to emanate. Add the sherry, lobster stock and cream, and bring to a boil. Simmer for 10 minutes. Allow to cool slightly. In a food processor, liquidize the mixture until a smooth sauce is formed. Return to heat and reduce until thickened. Season to taste. Coat each swordfish steak with seasoned flour. In a large sauté pan, sauté the fish steaks until golden brown. Deglaze the pan with a splash of white wine and add the sauce. Bake in a casserole in a 350-degree oven for 10 minutes. Serves 6.

THE GREAT OUTDOORS TRADING
COMPANY AND CAFE
High Springs

THE GREAT OUTDOORS TRADING COMPANY AND CAFE

In the tiny town of High Springs, just northwest of Gainesville, there is a small cafe where some very innovative food is being served.

Rob and Leslie Justis, formerly canoe outfitters on the Withlacoochee River, opened their Great Outdoors Trading Company a few years ago in a brick, two-story building on the main block of town. Constructed as an opera house in 1895 and '96 when the town was booming from the railroad and phosphate mining, the building was the hub of the community for years. Stage performances, silent films and dances drew crowds to the second floor, and a mercantile store sold all sorts of goods on the first floor.

The Justises restored the original heart-pine floors, removed the stucco to expose the brick walls and proceeded to sell camping equipment and apparel. When the attached one-story building, constructed as a barbershop in 1915, became available, they put a door through the wall, renovated and expanded into the restaurant business.

The Justises are committed to serving natural, unadulterated food that not only tastes good, but is good for you. They don't have a microwave oven or a deep-fat fryer on the premises. Everything they prepare is fresh; they refuse to purchase even frozen chickens. Their biscuits are made using only whole-wheat flour. A vegetarian special is offered at every meal along with their regular menu. Blessedly, no smoking is permitted.

But this is not just a health food restaurant. The menu contains a wide variety of broiled seafood, interesting soups and salads, fresh vegetables, chicken dishes and desserts like Hazelnut Torte and Chocolate Mousse. Their cholesterol-free tofu dishes, such as Tofu Florentine and the Sizzler sandwich have won over the tastes of even die-hard meat-and-potato eaters.

When I was there for Sunday brunch, I enjoyed their fish chowder and a tofu Ocean Delight Omelet, filled with shrimp, scallops and Cheddar cheese. Their wonderful grits are the result of accidentally putting Spike seasoning in the pot one morning; the grits were so tasty they've done it ever since.

It's easy to understand why visitors who come from every state in the Union and many European countries for canoeing, fishing and the best cave diving in the world have signed the guest register here. The friendly small-town atmosphere, the mellow old building and the wholesome good food make the Great Outdoors a great place to be.—B.R.M.

The Great Outdoors Trading Company and Cafe is located at 65-85 North Main Street in High Springs. Hours are from 11:30 a.m. until 9:00 p.m. Sunday through Thursday, and until 10:00 p.m. Friday and Saturday. Reservations are recommended; phone (904) 454-2900.

THE GREAT OUTDOORS CAFE'S JAMAICAN CHICKEN NOUVELLE

1 large shrimp
½ boneless chicken breast
Spike to taste
black pepper to taste

2 tomato slices
¼ avocado, sliced thin
¼ cup hollandaise sauce

Poach the shrimp and split it lengthwise; set aside. Pound chicken with a mallet until very thin. Broil chicken breast, topped with Spike and pepper. When it is nearly done, remove chicken from broiler and top with tomato slices, avocado slices and shrimp. Place in a 450-degree oven for 1 to 2 minutes. Top with hollandaise sauce. Serves 1.

THE GREAT OUTDOORS CAFE'S TOFU SALAD DRESSING

½ cup apple cider vinegar
½ cup tamari (natural soy sauce)
1½ cups vegetable oil

½ teaspoon fresh basil
1 pound fresh tofu
2 cloves garlic
¼ cup chopped onions

Mix all the ingredients in a blender until puréed. Serve over salads. Yields 3½ to 4 cups.

51

THE GREAT OUTDOORS CAFE'S CLAM CHOWDER

1 large onion, chopped
1 tablespoon butter
½ ounce Spike seasoning
¼ teaspoon black pepper,
   freshly ground
¼ teaspoon Tabasco sauce
¼ teaspoon ground
   rosemary
⅛ teaspoon celery salt

½ teaspoon thyme
1 baked potato
1 pint heavy cream
1 pint half-and-half
1 baked potato, cubed
1 pound clams, chopped
2 tablespoons finely
   chopped parsley
2 ounces cooking sherry

Sauté onions in butter until transparent. Add seasonings to the onions. Mash the baked potato and blend it with cream and half-and-half. Add to the onion mixture and stir well. Add the potato cubes and clams to the chowder and heat over low heat until thoroughly cooked. (Clams should be almost rubbery.) Adjust seasonings to taste and add parsley and sherry. Serves 6.

THE PRIMROSE INN
Gainesville

THE PRIMROSE INN

Generations of University of Florida graduates remember eating at the Primrose Inn in Gainesville. Until recent years, when restaurant chains flooded in, the Primrose was the main eating establishment in this college town.

Built as a private home in the early part of this century, the frame and stone two-story house was purchased in 1924 by the Byron Winn, Sr., family. They made additions and turned it into a hotel and restaurant. Son Byron Winn, Jr., who became mayor of Gainesville in 1963, carried on the family tradition from the '40s to the '70s.

The present owner, Jack McCraw, a relaxed Alabama native, bought the Primrose in 1974. Though the Primrose no longer provides lodging, southern-style cooking continues to be served in a homey, friendly atmosphere.

A sofa and chairs beside the stone fireplace in the entrance hall provide an inviting spot to sit and wait and talk with friends, or for the regulars to catch up on each other's news. The Primrose is busiest during the week, when businesspeople and college professors come for lunch, and after church on Sunday.

The day I visited the Primrose Inn, I was invited to the kitchen to talk with the head cook, Arthur Robinson, who has been at the Primrose Inn since he got out of the army in 1945. He and Boston Cobb, who has been at the Primrose for twenty years, turn out fifteen hundred of the inn's famous Yeast Rolls a day.

From a menu that includes such traditional favorites as Country Steak with Onions, Roast Round of Beef, Baked Sugar-cured Ham, Fried Seafood Platter and Smothered Chicken with Yellow Rice, I ordered the Salmon Croquettes and the delicious Squash Casserole. And I had to have some of their Southern Fried Chicken, which reminded me of Sunday at my grandmother's house many years ago.—B.R.M.

The Primrose Inn is located at 214 West University Avenue in Gainesville. Lunch is served from 11:30 a.m. to 2:20 p.m., and dinner is served from 5:00 p.m. to 8:45 p.m., Sunday through Friday. The restaurant is closed Saturday. Reservations are not accepted. For information call (904) 376-9348.

THE PRIMROSE INN'S SALMON CROQUETTES

1 15½-ounce can pink
  salmon
1 onion, chopped
2 eggs, beaten
½ teaspoon pepper
¼ teaspoon garlic salt

¼ teaspoon seasoning salt
½ cup or more instant
  mashed potato mix
2 cups or more vegetable
  oil

Drain the salmon. Mix together the salmon, onions, eggs and seasonings, adding potato mix to tighten. Roll into small cakes about the size of half dollars. Deep-fry in oil for a few minutes until brown. Serves 4.

THE PRIMROSE INN'S SQUASH CASSEROLE

2 pounds yellow squash
1 stick butter (or margarine)
2 eggs
1 tablespoon grated Par-
  mesan cheese
1 small onion, chopped

1 small green pepper,
  chopped
¼ teaspoon pepper
¼ teaspoon seasoning salt
½ cup grated American
  cheese

Cook the squash until tender; drain and mash. Cut the butter into small chunks. Mix together all the ingredients except the American cheese. Place in an ungreased casserole and top with American cheese. Cook 15 to 20 minutes in a 350-degree oven until the eggs gel. Serves 6.

THE PRIMROSE INN'S YEAST ROLLS

1 package of yeast
½ cup or more warm water
2 eggs
4 cups plain flour, sifted
2 cups warm milk

1 stick butter, melted (or
  margarine)
1 cup white sugar
1 cup flour
1 tablespoon butter, melted

Dissolve yeast in warm water. Add eggs to yeast mixture. To the quart of flour, add milk, the yeast and egg mixture, then the melted butter and the sugar. Use another cup or so of flour to tighten the dough enough to roll out; cut with a biscuit cutter or the rim of a glass. Place rolls on a greased pan and brush with melted butter. Bake at 350 degrees until brown, 15 to 20 minutes or so. Serves 8 to 10.

THE SOVEREIGN RESTAURANT
Gainesville

THE SOVEREIGN RESTAURANT

One hundred years ago, blacksmiths were shoeing horses in the livery stable which is now the Sovereign Restaurant. Built in 1879 as an adjunct to the opera house next door, the yellow brick building changed with the times. It served as a warehouse, a machine shop and a garage before being converted into the inviting restaurant it is today.

Located near the restored town square of Gainesville and the Hippodrome State Theater, the Sovereign fits well into its surroundings. A handsome, iron gate opens from the street to allow diners to enter the restaurant via a brick alleyway that hints of New Orleans. The interior is highlighted with a lovely cathedral ceiling, stained glass, rich wood and paisley tablecloths. An enclosed patio, with original brick floors, features Victorian antiques, including a marble-topped shoe-shine stand.

Elmo Moser, who was born in the Swiss Alps and trained as an executive chef, has been running the Sovereign for ten years. His menu offerings range from Beef Wellington, Saltimbocca and Chicken Jerusalem to Red Snapper Meunière, with daily specials. On Wednesdays, his wife Lupe prepares Mexican dishes, which he says are "always very authentic and always very popular."

Moser encouraged me to try his Scallone a la Sovereign, an entrée of abalone and scallops sautéed with mushrooms. He told me his is one of the few restaurants on the East Coast to serve this since the abalone must be flown in from California. After tasting this specialty, I could understand the pride he takes in it.

I also enjoyed tasting his Beef Cayenne, with its spicy sauce of cream and cayenne pepper, though it is definitely for those who like it hot. But no matter. The Margarita Pie, made with Lupe's secret recipe, brought soothing relief. No amount of cajolery could enduce them to reveal the recipe, but that just gives me one more excuse to visit again.—B.R.M.

The Sovereign Restaurant is located at 12 Southeast Second Avenue in Gainesville. Lunch hours are 11:00 a.m. to 2:00 p.m.

Monday through Friday; dinner hours are from 5:30 to 10:00 p.m. Monday through Thursday, and from 5:30 to 11:00 p.m. on Friday and Saturday. The restaurant is closed Sunday. For reservations (recommended) call (904) 378-6307.

THE SOVEREIGN RESTAURANT'S SHRIMP ANDERSON

20 ounces frozen leaf
  spinach, thawed
2 tablespoons butter
garlic salt to taste
salt and pepper to taste
24 large shrimp, peeled and
  deveined
4 shallots, chopped
juice of half a lemon or
  more

splash of white wine
8 black olives, pitted and
  sliced
8 green olives, pitted and
  sliced
4 ounces Swiss cheese,
  grated
4 ounces blue cheese,
  grated

Sauté the spinach with butter, garlic salt, salt and pepper. Place in an au gratin platter and hold warm. In a second skillet, sauté the shrimp with salt, pepper, butter and shallots until lightly done. Add a little lemon juice and white wine. Place sautéed shrimp on top of spinach, sprinkle with olives and mixed cheeses and bake in a 375-degree oven for 5 minutes. Serve hot with rice or boiled potatoes. Serves 4.

THE SOVEREIGN RESTAURANT'S BEEF CAYENNE

24 ounces sliced beef
  tenderloin
salt to taste
1 to 2 teaspoons cayenne
  pepper

½ cup flour
¼ cup white wine
1 cup heavy cream
4 ounces sliced almonds

Put sliced tenderloin on a plate and lightly dust with salt, cayenne pepper and flour. Sauté in a hot skillet until medium rare. Sprinkle the beef with white wine, then add heavy cream and almonds and bring to a boil. Serve immediately with rice or noodles. Serves 4.

THE SOVEREIGN RESTAURANT'S BROWNIE PIE

3 ounces semisweet
  chocolate morsels
8 ounces sugar
2 whole eggs
1 egg yolk
3½ ounces butter, softened

dash of vanilla
2 ounces all-purpose flour,
  sifted
½ cup heavy cream
1 cup graham cracker
  crumbs

In a double boiler, slowly melt chocolate morsels over low heat. In a mixing bowl, add sugar, eggs, egg yolk, soft butter and a dash of vanilla. Whip until fluffy. Fold in melted chocolate, flour and heavy cream and stir to incorporate. Butter a 9-inch pie pan well and sprinkle it with graham cracker crumbs. Fill with brownie mixture. Bake for 30 minutes at 325 degrees. Serves 8 to 10.

THE ISLAND HOTEL
Cedar Key

THE ISLAND HOTEL

You don't just stumble across the Island Hotel. You drive for miles through rural countryside and marshland to reach the island of Cedar Key, located on the Gulf halfway between Tallahassee and St. Petersburg.

Artists, fishermen and vacationers in the know have already discovered the joys of this quaint community, likened by some to a Key West of twenty years ago.

Before the Civil War, the town of Cedar Key prospered in its role as the western terminus for the first cross-Florida railroad, which linked the Gulf to Fernandina Beach on the Atlantic. The Island Hotel, listed on the National Register of Historic Places, was built here in 1849. It was here when the Yankees occupied Cedar Key in 1862. It was here when the lumber boom of the 1880s consumed the island's abundant cedar trees for the manufacture of pencils. It survived the devastating hurricane and tidal wave of 1896. And it remained as the depletion of natural resources and a competing railroad made progress pass on by.

Built of three-foot-thick walls of tabby, the two-story hotel was designed to catch breezes and has a wraparound porch on which to enjoy them. Along the upstairs hall of the hotel is a wall mural painted in 1896 by an unknown artist. Another artist painted a mural over the hotel bar in the 1940s.

The Island Hotel is currently owned by Marcia Rogers, a psychologist who operated a natural foods restaurant in Vermont before visiting Florida. She walked into the hotel on April Fools' Day in 1980 and just sensed that it was meant for her. She bought the hotel and has been running it as a caring oasis ever since.

Her restaurant reflects her personal philosophy, emphasizing the wholesome and natural. All the food is fresh, with no preservatives or additives. Herbs are picked from her own garden. No meats are served and the microwave is forbidden here.

The restaurant is known for its wonderful seafood and vegetable specialties, served with brown rice. The Baked Fish and Garlic Shrimp have won critical acclaim, as has the Artichokes Atsena Otie, named for a nearby key. I found the blackened fish of the day, amberjack, to be delicious, as were the Stuffed Mushroom Caps. The homemade Poppyseed Bread was excellent.

The dining room is unpretentious and relaxing, with classical background music soothing the ear and spirit. Rogers' personal art collection adorns the walls; fresh flowers brighten the tables. The orginal wood floors creak and have their ups and downs in a testimony to age. The Island Hotel is ungussied-up Old Florida at its most authentic.—B.R.M.

The Island Hotel is located at 2nd and B Streets in Cedar Key. Wednesday through Sunday, dinner is served from 6:00 to 10:00 p.m. The restaurant is closed Monday and Tuesday. For reservations (recommended) call (904) 543-5111.

THE ISLAND HOTEL'S FISH AND PASTRY

3 sections filo dough (can be bought frozen)
1 6- to 8-ounce grouper fillet, cleaned
¼ cup hot Japanese mustard
¼ cup mayonnaise
¼ teaspoon white pepper
½ cup sparkling mineral water
1 tablespoon butter, melted

Thaw filo dough completely in the refrigerator, always keeping it covered well to prevent its drying out. Cut the fish into 3 sections. Keep the grouper on a plate of ice while preparing other ingredients to prevent flavor and nutrition loss. Mix mustard and mayonnaise and add white pepper. Dry the fish fillet and cut it into 1-by-3-inch strips. Dip fish in sparkling mineral water, then in mustard-mayonnaise sauce. Brush filo leaves with melted butter. Place a piece of fish on top of each pastry leaf, and wrap each like an envelope. Bake on a wire rack in a pan at 350 degrees until pastry is browned (pastry won't brown until fish is cooked). Do not microwave. Serves 1.

THE ISLAND HOTEL'S FISH ISLAND HOTEL

1 4- to 8-ounce fresh fish
fillet or fish steak (shark,
grouper, drum or other
nonoily light fish)
1 tablespoon chopped fresh
herbs (thyme, parsley,
basil or dill)

¼ teaspoon Spike
seasoning
¼ cup sesame seeds,
toasted
¼ cup white wine
4 tablespoons clarified
butter

Place fish in a glass pan. Sprinkle with fresh herbs and
Spike. Cover almost completely with sesame seeds. Mix the
wine and butter and pour over the fish, covering the bottom of
the pan no more than ¼-inch deep. Bake at 350 degrees for 10
to 15 minutes, until the fish is light and puffy. Do not microwave. Serves 1.

THE ISLAND HOTEL'S GARLIC SHRIMP

16 to 20 fresh shrimp
whole head of garlic cloves,
minced
½ stick butter, clarified

1 teaspoon fresh dill
¼ teaspoon Spike
seasoning

Peel, devein and butterfly the shrimp; place them on a plate
of ice. Allow the minced garlic to sit in clarified butter several
minutes before heating. Place in sauté pan and bring up the
heat, but don't smoke. Add the shrimp, dill and Spike seasoning. Leave the shrimp on one side; don't turn them. Watch
closely, and when the shrimp lose their transparency, turn the
heat off and put a cover on the pan. To serve, place the shrimp
on plates and pour bits of garlic over them. Serves 2.

FIRST AND BROADWAY
Ocala

FIRST AND BROADWAY

At First and Broadway in Ocala, a town known for its rolling hills and beautiful horse farms, the building is old but the management style is new.

First and Broadway is located in a three-story brick building constructed in 1885 as the Ocala Opera House. Known as the Marion Block Building, it was for many years an office building and drugstore. Randolph Tucker and the actor Patrick O'Neal and his brother Michael rehabilitated the building in 1980, opening the O'Neal Bros. restaurant in 1981. In the summer of 1987, it was purchased by Dale Twardowski, and the name changed to First and Broadway, indicating its location on the corner of First Avenue and Broadway.

Left intact at the entrance to the restaurant are the hexagonal tiles of the old drugstore. Wood planking is painted a dark green on the walls, topped with exposed bricks. Brass rails, potted palms and bentwood chairs add to the nostalgic décor.

Managers Don Kisselbach and Rich Bianculli, with experience in New York restaurants and Disney World, were hired in 1986 to bolster business. They added green awnings to the exterior and removed the carpeting to expose the now-beautiful hardwood floors. And then they set out to "lighten the stuffy atmosphere."

Waiters no longer serve in tuxedos; they wear striped shirts and suspenders. Waiters and waitresses receive three weeks of training in different aspects of food and liquor service and then must pass a test.

The menu was enlarged to more than a hundred selections, designed to appeal to "both beer and champagne tastes." In keeping with the grazing trend so popular today, twenty-four appetizers are offered, ranging from vegetable turnovers, nachos, cheese melts and conch fritters to country pâté and escargots.

Numerous soups, salads, sandwiches and desserts are featured, as are omelets, pasta and classic entrées like Steak Oscar, Beef Wellington and Seafood Newburg. I especially enjoyed the delicious Tortellini Pesto I sampled. A different drink is featured daily, with more than three hundred specialty drinks available. A champagne brunch is served on Sunday.

Customers can buy any item at any time of the day or night, and the menu changes every six months. The restaurant takes pride in offering fast service for lunch so that people can get back to work. Plans were underway when I visited to open a sidewalk cafe in the front, overlooking the fountain and palm trees of the town square.

By using many of the marketing techniques of popular chain restaurants, and by cooking fresh food prepared in-house, which many chains don't do, First and Broadway seems to have found a winning combination: business doubled this past year.—B.R.M.

First and Broadway is located at 24 Southeast Broadway in Ocala. Hours are from 11:30 a.m. to 1:00 a.m. Monday through Thursday, and until 2:00 a.m. on Friday and Saturday. Sunday brunch is served from 11:00 a.m. to 3:00 p.m. Reservations are accepted but are not required; phone (904) 351-5532.

FIRST AND BROADWAY'S TORTELLINI PESTO

9 ounces mixed tortellini
2 tablespoons butter
8 ounces heavy cream

2 ounces grated Parmesan cheese
1 to 3 tablespoons Pesto Sauce (recipe below)

Cook tortellini according to package directions. Rinse and drain pasta. Place butter and heavy cream in skillet. Bring to a boil. Add tortellini, grated cheese and Pesto Sauce. Cook for 60 seconds. Serve hot. Serves 1 to 2.

Pesto Sauce:

4 cups fresh basil, tightly packed
½ cup olive oil
½ bunch fresh parsley
1 tablespoon garlic

¼ cup pine nuts
½ cup Parmesan cheese
½ teaspoon salt
½ teaspoon pepper

Blend all the ingredients in a food processor until puréed. Refrigerate the sauce until you are ready to use it. Yields 1½ cups.

FIRST AND BROADWAY'S CHICKEN WALNUT SALAD

1 pint diced celery
1 pint chopped orange
  sections
1¼ cups chopped English
  walnuts
¼ cup chopped parsley
1 pint mayonnaise

1 teaspoon salt
½ teaspoon white pepper
½ cup chopped yellow
  onions
1½ pounds chicken breasts,
  poached

Mix together all the ingredients except the chicken. Dice chicken into ¾-inch pieces. Add chicken to mixture and toss with a rubber spatula to maintain whole pieces; do not mash the chicken. Serves 12.

FIRST AND BROADWAY'S CHOCOLATE CHEESECAKE

Crust:

1½ cups graham cracker
  crumbs
1 tablespoon cinnamon

1 tablespoon sugar
2 tablespoons butter,
  melted

Mix graham cracker crumbs with cinnamon, sugar and melted butter. Press the mixture into a 9-inch springform pan.

Filling:

2½ pounds cream cheese
½ ounce lemon juice
1 ounce Cointreau liqueur
1 tablespoon vanilla extract
1 ounce crème de cocoa
  (white)

6 tablespoons butter
3 ounces flour
1 pound confectioners'
  sugar
8 eggs
1 cup sour cream

Beat cream cheese until soft and smooth. Add lemon juice, liqueur, vanilla, crème de cocoa, butter, flour and confectioners' sugar and cream together. Beat in eggs and sour cream last. Pour into a cheesecake pan lined with graham cracker mix. Place pan in a water bath on a sheet pan. Bake at 350 degrees for 1¼ hours. Yields 1 cheesecake.

THE LAKESIDE INN
Mount Dora

THE LAKESIDE INN   **D**riving up to the Lakeside Inn on the shore of Lake Dora, thirty miles from Orlando, you breathe a sigh of contentment. Left behind are the city traffic and crowds, the tight schedules and frayed nerves. Here, in a town of quiet, hilly streets with lovely old homes and antique shops, at an inn with front-porch rocking chairs and enormous oaks draped with Spanish moss, the soul can restore itself.

The Lakeside Inn was built in 1883 as a ten-room hotel called the Alexander House. The country resort attracted northern visitors eager for wintertime warmth and for the exotic wildlife and scenery found among Lake County's fourteen hundred lakes.

In the 1920s, the inn was in its heyday, offering popular music and entertainment and boating excursions. President Calvin Coolidge, who dedicated the hotel's two new wings in 1930, spent the winter at the inn after his term of office ended.

Listed on the National Register of Historic Places, the Lakeside Inn has just undergone a $4 million award-winning restoration. Ellison Ketchum, who operated the Martha Washington Inn in Virginia and the Belvedere in Baltimore, supervised the rejuvenation.

He is proud of the fact the owners did not gut the interior, and that they restored the original wood floors and window casings. Thirty-two coats of paint had to be removed from the exterior of the spacious frame hotel before it was painted Flagler yellow. Though thoroughly modernized, with new tennis courts and a redone 1920s Olympic-sized pool, the hotel has retained its original character.

A wide variety of fare is offered in the handsome Beauclaire Dining Room. Chicken Alfredo, Shrimp Feta, Steak Diane du Chef, Fresh Pan-fried Trout and Veal Chasseur are just a few of the selections. All the food is fresh and prepared to order, with innovative specials daily.

My own pleasurable dinner began with a smooth, cold Peaches and Cream Soup. The house salad was served with flair in a whole head of Boston lettuce filled with crunchy vegetables. Unusual and delicious was the Fried Bread, the result of an experiment by Ellison Ketchum. The Shepherd's Pie, made with tenderloin tips and served piping hot in a crock, was the best I've ever tasted.

Over dinner, as background classical music played, I learned about the special events sponsored by the inn, like the annual antique boat show in March and the Agatha Christie-style "mystery weekends." The ambiance and cuisine of the Lakeside Inn are conducive to a leisurely meal with good conversation.—B.R.M.

The Lakeside Inn is located at 100 South Alexander Street in Mount Dora. Breakfast hours are from 7:00 a.m. to 10:30 a.m. daily. Lunch hours are from 11:30 a.m. to 2:30 p.m. Monday through Friday, and from noon to 2:30 p.m. on Saturday and Sunday. Dinner is served from 6:00 to 8:00 p.m. Sunday through Thursday, and until 9:00 p.m. Friday and Saturday. Reservations are suggested; phone (904) 383-4101.

THE LAKESIDE INN'S CARPETBAGGER

6 8-ounce filets mignon	**1 stick sweet butter**
1 pint fresh oysters	**6 slices bacon**
1 tablespoon fresh chopped	**1 cup heavy cream**
shallots	**lemon pepper to taste**
2 stalks celery, chopped	

Cut a pocket in each filet, then set aside. Sauté oysters, shallots and chopped celery in a little of the butter. When oysters are done, remove from heat. Stuff 2 oysters and some of the celery mixture into each filet; wrap each with a slice of bacon and secure with toothpicks. Grill filets to desired doneness. Heat remaining oyster mixture with heavy cream; cook until the liquid is reduced by half. Add lemon pepper. Whip in the remaining butter until sauce is smooth; serve sauce over filets. (If sauce is too thin, add a little cornstarch roux.) Serves 6.

71

THE LAKESIDE INN'S PEACHES AND CREAM SOUP

12 large peaches, very ripe
¼ cup orange blossom
  honey
2 cinnamon sticks

8 cups heavy whipping
  cream
Napoleon brandy to taste
1 teaspoon nutmeg

Remove skin and pits from peaches and purée in a food processor or blender. Pour purée into a large mixing bowl; add remaining ingredients and stir. Check sweetness by taste and add more honey if necessary. Refrigerate to chill. Remove cinnamon sticks just before serving and serve chilled. Serves 8 to 10.

THE LAKESIDE INN'S BANANA SPLIT TORTE

2 11-ounce boxes vanilla
  wafers
4 sticks butter, melted
¼ cup sugar
3 eggs
24 ounces confectioners'
  sugar
1 24-ounce bottle chocolate
  syrup

1 20-ounce can crushed
  pineapple
6 to 8 bananas
2 cups whipping cream,
  whipped
½ cup maraschino cherries
1 cup chopped walnuts

Crush vanilla wafers and mix with 1 cup of the melted butter and the granulated sugar. Grease a 9-by-13- by-2-inch pan and spread wafer mixture on bottom of the pan to form a crust. Whip the eggs, the remaining cup of melted butter and the powdered sugar until creamy and pour evenly over crust. Top with chocolate syrup to form the next layer. Drain pineapple and spread over mixture. Slice the bananas and layer over top. Cover with whipped cream and garnish with cherries and walnuts. Put the torte in the freezer for 24 hours. Prior to serving, place in the refrigerator to thaw enough to slice. Serves 8 to 12.

LA BELLE VERRIERE
Winter Park

LA BELLE VERRIERE

At La Belle Verrière, you dine surrounded by priceless works of art many museums would covet. The restaurant's name means "the beautiful stained glass," and the name is apt, though it doesn't begin to convey the wonder of this place.

Overlooking a verdant park in downtown Winter Park, this dining establishment is in a building that served for fifty years as Irvine's Drugstore. In 1976, interior designer Jeannette Genius McKean, granddaughter of the founder of Winter Park, and her husband, Hugh McKean, a former president of Rollins College, renovated the structure. They designed La Belle Verrière as a restaurant that would showcase their Art Nouveau stained glass.

In 1930, when he was a young artist, Hugh McKean studied under the aging Louis Comfort Tiffany at Laurelton Hall, Tiffany's famous Art Nouveau estate in Oyster Bay, New York, which burned in 1957. McKean's collection of Tiffany's stained-glass windows, lamps and vases—now displayed in the Charles Morse Museum within a block of the restaurant—is the world's largest.

There are four dining areas in La Belle Verrière, each unique. In the Fernery, a beautiful Louis Tiffany window now graces a contemporary setting. The centerpiece of the main dining room is the famous Peacock Window. It was pointed out to me that as in most Tiffany works, no color was applied to the surface of the glass with enameling; instead the glass was colored by the addition of metallic oxides when in a molten state. Tiffany's Daffodil Window, three panels of Favrile glass from the Brown Renfro mansion in Pennsylvania, and a panel from the First Presbyterian Church of Hoboken, New Jersey are also included in this restaurant's extraordinary assemblage.

Another dining area spotlights the Arts Window, an excellent example of enameled glass, created by the artist Frederick Lamb and shown at expositions in 1895 and 1902. Abel Landry, a leading Parisian designer at the turn of the century, is honored in still another room, which is designed around his stained-glass mirror panel.

La Belle Verrière is a lovely, thought-inspiring setting in which to dine on classic French cuisine. The menu offers a well-rounded selection of fresh seafood, veal, steaks, fowl and rack of lamb, with tempting desserts and international coffees.

When I was there for lunch, I sampled their Gratinée au Brie, a soup that has won them fame, and found it delicious. And never being one to skimp even when I should, I had to have the Mousse au Chocolat, a rich and wonderful dessert.— B.R.M.

La Belle Verrière is located at 142 Park Avenue South in Winter Park. Lunch is served from 11:30 a.m. to 2:30 p.m. and dinner from 6:00 to 10:00 p.m., Monday through Saturday. Reservations are recommended; phone (305) 645-3377.

LA BELLE VERRIERE'S GRATINEE AU BRIE

1 cup finely diced onions	2 tablespoons butter
½ cup finely diced leeks	½ cup heavy cream, heated
2 tablespoons butter	salt and pepper to taste
1 cup veal stock	4 to 6 slices French bread
1 cup chicken stock	(or toast rounds)
2 tablespoons flour	8 ounces Brie cheese

Sauté onions and leeks lightly in butter. Add veal and chicken stocks; simmer until tender. Mix flour and melted butter to make a roux; add to sauté pan, thickening stock with roux until it is the consistency of light gravy. Simmer 10 minutes; add heated heavy cream, salt and pepper. Pour soup into crockery bowls; top each bowl with a thin slice of French bread or toast rounds spread with a generous amount of Brie cheese. Place in a 450-degree oven or under the broiler until cheese is melted and lightly browned. Serves 4 to 6.

LA BELLE VERRIERE'S MOUSSE AU CHOCOLAT

**14 1-ounce squares semi-
   sweet chocolate
1 quart heavy whipping
   cream**

**15 egg yolks
¾ cup sugar
¼ cup Triple Sec liqueur**

Melt chocolate in the top of a double boiler. In a mixing
bowl, beat whipping cream until it peaks; refrigerate. Put egg
yolks and sugar in another mixing bowl; beat with mixer until
very thick. When thick, beat in chocolate by hand. Add Triple
Sec. Fold in whipped cream. Refrigerate the mousse overnight. Serves 15.

PARK PLAZA GARDENS
Winter Park

PARK PLAZA GARDENS

Adjoining the beautifully restored, European-style Park Plaza Hotel in Winter Park is a culinary gem, Park Plaza Gardens. The building now housing the restaurant was constructed in 1926. It was for years a Winn-Lovett grocery store, then a Winn-Dixie. The original oak icebox can still be seen today, functioning as the refrigerator for the bar.

In what used to be a service entrance of the hotel, an enclosed brick courtyard has been built. The ficus trees, calla lilies and fresh potted flowers create a lovely greenhouse for dining.

Tom Lutz, who opened the Park Plaza Gardens in 1979, is a Floridian who started working in restaurants when he was twelve. After graduating from Cornell Hotel School, he worked with a hotel firm in Germany, catering the Olympics in Munich. Many of the touches he learned in Europe are apparent in his restaurant now.

The creator of the culinary style at Park Plaza Gardens is chef Emile Benel. When he was first hired by the restaurant, he was eighty-three years old, with credentials that included cooking for the Plaza Hotel, the Mayflower and five United States presidents. Now in his nineties, and retired, he and Lutz are writing a book about his life and recipes.

To continue its tradition of innovative cooking, the Park Plaza Gardens has an exchange program with the world-famous Palace Hotel in Gestaad, Switzerland. The restaurants swap two chefs for three to six months a year.

It's small wonder then that their menu affords such a tempting variety. Dishes range from Oyster Salad Florentine to Swordfish Scallopini, from Veal Curry Chiffonade to Pheasant Perigourdine. Seafood receives particular emphasis, with twenty-two seafood entrées. A special list of low-cholesterol, low-sodium dishes, approved by the American Heart Association, is also offered.

The lunch I shared with Lutz was a taste-tester's dream. I began with a spicy Cajun Crayfish Bisque, followed by a beautifully prepared veal salad. I didn't want to stop eating the Fisherman's Pie, but was encouraged to try the Red Snapper Bretonne, guaranteed to win over the most determined steak lover. The secret of this fabulous dish is the doubly reduced glace de viande sauce, and the absolutely fresh fish. Chef Valentin Schwaegerl says they prepare their own glace de viande by reducing a gallon of veal stock to ½-ounce of all-meat syrup. I was told that large commercial fishing boats often ice "fresh" fish down for ten days before coming ashore; Park Plaza Gardens buys its supply from a fisherman on the dock and prepares the fish within twenty-four hours of their being caught.

At the risk of being labeled a gourmand rather than a gourmet, I agreed to take "just a bite" of their renowned caramel custard. It was pure bliss.—B.R.M.

Park Plaza Gardens is located at 319 Park Avenue South in Winter Park. Monday through Saturday, breakfast is served from 8:00 a.m. to 11:00 a.m.; lunch is served from 11:30 a.m. to 3:00 p.m. Dinner hours are from 6:00 p.m. to 10:00 p.m. Sunday through Thursday, and until 11:00 p.m. on Friday and Saturday. Sunday brunch is served from 11:00 a.m. to 3:00 p.m. Reservations are recommended; phone (305) 645-2475.

PARK PLAZA GARDENS' FISHERMAN'S PIE

4 ounces Duchess potatoes (favorite recipe)
2 ounces dry white wine
2 ounces heavy cream
2 ounces fish stock
½ teaspoon chopped shallots
6 ounces assorted seafood (shrimp, scallops, lobster, crab, fish pieces)

lemon juice to taste
salt and cayenne pepper to taste
2 tablespoons hollandaise sauce
2 ounces grated fontinella cheese

With a pastry bag and star tube, pipe duchess potatoes around the edge of a shallow, 12-ounce ceramic casserole dish, so that the potatoes will encircle the pie filling. Place dish in a 350-degree oven for 3 minutes to brown the potatoes; remove from oven and set aside. Combine wine, cream, fish stock and shallots and bring to a boil. Add seafood and poach 2 minutes. Remove fish and shellfish and reduce liquid to light cream consistency; season with lemon, salt and cayenne to taste. Remove from heat and blend the cheese and hollandaise sauce. Return fish to cream mixture and pour into the casserole dish with the browned potatoes and serve. Serves 1.

PARK PLAZA GARDENS' RED SNAPPER BRETONNE

1 6-ounce fillet of fresh red
  snapper
2 tablespoons flour
salt and pepper to taste
2 ounces clarified butter
½ teaspoon glace de viande
½ teaspoon chopped
  parsley

dash of lemon juice
2 tablespoons whole butter
2 ounces fresh mushrooms,
  quartered
½ teaspoon capers
1 lemon wedge for garnish

Dredge the fish fillet in flour seasoned with salt and pepper, and shake off excess. Sauté fish in hot clarified butter for approximately 1 minute on each side, depending on the thickness of fish. Remove fish to a hot plate and drizzle glace de viande over top. Sprinkle chopped parsley and lemon juice on top of fish. Melt the whole butter in a pan and sauté mushrooms for 1 minute. Remove mushrooms and place on top of fish with capers. Bring butter remaining in the pan to a light brown stage over high heat and splash this foaming butter over fish. Serve extremely hot with a fresh lemon wedge. Serves 1.

LILI MARLENE'S
AVIATORS PUB AND RESTAURANT
Orlando

LILI MARLENE'S AVIATORS PUB AND RESTAURANT

At Church Street Station in Orlando, the good times roll in a merry mix of food, drink and entertainment modeled after days past.

Centered around the old train station in downtown Orlando's historic district, Church Street Station fills more than a block on both sides of the street. The old depot, flanked by an antique steam engine on the tracks beside it, now houses antique and gift shops. A glorious Old West saloon, a hot-air balloon museum and numerous bars and stores are anchored by Lili Marlene's Aviators Pub and Restaurant.

In the evening, the street is closed to traffic, while antique cars, horse-drawn buggies, jugglers and mimes create a carnivallike atmosphere. An admission fee charged after 5:00 p.m. admits you to the complex and to all the live shows, featuring country-and-western and Dixieland music, as well as vaudeville and cancan acts.

Lili Marlene's Aviators Pub and Restaurant is a painstaking rejuvenation of the Strand Hotel, built in 1922. The restaurant glows with antique treasures, collected by owner and entrepreneur Bob Snow during his world travels. The oak and beveled-glass doorway is from the famous Pace home in Pensacola. The heart-pine floors came from an old warehouse in New Orleans. The hand-carved oak booths where diners now sit were church pews in a French Catholic church; the telephone booth was an oak confessional. The beautiful forty-foot bar and solid brass fans were recovered from a doomed Philadelphia hotel. The sixty-foot brass railing, made in 1903 and weighing five thousand pounds, came from the First National Bank of Atlanta.

In addition to this stunning array, authentic aviation memorabilia from World War I to the present day is suspended from the ceiling. Early radio broadcasts and the Lili Marlene World War II ballad are played in the background as diners bask in the nostalgia of it all.

The restaurant offers a wide range of lunch and dinner selections, specializing in Blackened Prime Rib and fresh Florida seafood. An extensive wine list is offered, as are flamboyant drinks like the Strawberry Daiquiri I indulged in.

For dinner, I enjoyed a scrumptious Scallop Mousseline and sampled the unusually good Baked Brie with Raspberry Vinaigrette. The special of the day, Veal Tips with Mushrooms and Burgundy Cream Sauce, was superb. After the delicious Chocolate Sponge Cake, I reluctantly had to race to the airport for my plane home. I would love to have lingered and viewed all the shows of Church Street Station.—B.R.M.

Lili Marlene's Aviators Pub and Restaurant is located in Church Street Station at 129 West Church Street in Orlando. Lunch is served daily from 11:00 a.m. to 4:00 p.m. and includes brunch items on Saturday and Sunday; dinner is served daily from 5:30 p.m. to midnight. Reservations are accepted; call (305) 422-2434.

LILI MARLENE'S AVIATORS PUB AND RESTAURANT'S CHICKEN, AVOCADO AND BACON SALAD

2 to 3 lettuce leaves
4½ ounces cooked white
  chicken meat, diced
½ ounce crisply cooked
  bacon, chopped
½ ounce diced avocado

Tarragon Dressing (recipe
  follows)
2 avocado slices
seasonal fruit for garnish
1 tablespoon mango
  chutney

Line a plate with leaf lettuce. Mix chicken with some of the chopped bacon and the diced avocado and Tarragon Dressing. Place this mixture in the center of the plate and top with the rest of the bacon and the avocado slices. Arrange fruit around the edges of the plate; accompany with mango chutney. Serves 1.

Tarragon Dressing:
2 ounces olive oil
1 ounce tarragon vinegar
1 teaspoon lemon juice

2 teaspoons Dijon mustard
1 tablespoon fresh tarragon
salt and pepper to taste

Whip all the ingredients together and pour over salad. Serves 1.

LILI MARLENE'S AVIATORS PUB AND RESTAURANT'S
BAKED BRIE WITH RASPBERRY VINAIGRETTE

3-ounce wedge Brie cheese
1 leaf puff pastry dough
1 egg yolk
1 tablespoon water
¼ ounce clarified butter
1 leaf of kale (optional)

1½ ounces Raspberry Vin-
    aigrette Dressing (recipe
    below)
1 strawberry, hulled
2 slices kiwi fruit

Wrap Brie in puff pastry dough. Beat egg yolk with a little water for an egg wash. Dip pastry-wrapped Brie in egg wash. Brush baking pan with clarified butter; add Brie and bake at 350 degrees until done, about 5 to 7 minutes. If desired, place a leaf of kale on a plate. Ladle vinaigrette onto plate; place Brie on top. Garnish with whole strawberry and kiwi slices. Serves 1.

Raspberry Vinaigrette Dressing:

1 egg yolk
1½ cups vegetable oil
1⅙ cups raspberry vinegar

⅛ cup chopped shallots
salt and pepper to taste

Whip egg yolk until creamy. Add oil, then vinegar. Add shallots and seasonings and mix well. Store leftover dressing in the refrigerator; shake well before using. Yields 2½ cups.

CHALET SUZANNE
Lake Wales

CHALET SUZANNE Driving down Highway 17-A, in the middle of Florida citrus country, you'll suddenly see what appears to be a mirage. Reflected in a shimmering lake is the image of a pastel-colored European village. Even after blinking, the image will remain. So, if you're the curious type, you'll steer your car down a brick pathway toward the image. And you'll discover the Hinshaw's eclectically decorated country inn and restaurant, Chalet Suzanne.

In 1931, at the height of the Great Depression, the widowed Bertha Hinshaw ignored the skeptics who didn't believe that people would go out of their way for exceptional food and lodging. She established Chalet Suzanne, and for over fifty years repeat guests have proved that culinary ingenuity and charm will generally find its audience.

Chalet Suzanne is a mélange of not exactly off-beat but off-measured buildings. After a fire, the Hinshaw's horse stable, rabbit hutch and chicken houses were patched together to form the meandering village. Whether painted pink or blue or lavender, you'll find the varied spiral- and rectangular-shaped buildings studded with ornamental ceramic tiles that define a corner, a window or a courtyard entrance. Bertha Hinshaw even preferred the beautiful tiles to tablecloths, so many of the dining room tables feature unusual tile patterns. Not only is each table top different, so are the sets of crystal, fine china, candlesticks and fresh floral arrangements.

Bertha's son Carl, a WWII Air Force pilot, inherited his late mother's culinary ability. His special soups have even been sent with the Apollo 15 and 16 crews to the moon. Their cannery will ship some soups home for you, too, if you like. Sitting with a view of the lake, I began my meal with Carl's creation of Cream of Romaine Soup and immediately understood why it is a NASA favorite. After consuming too many little Potato Rolls, I deglazed my palate with a Lemon and Champagne Sorbet. For my entrée, I was considering Shrimp Curry or Lobster Newburg until Carl's wife Vita advised that while Carl never gives out his recipe for Chicken Suzanne, I should try it anyway. I did, and was only sorry that I hadn't arrived hungrier, as they serve deliciously large portions. The Scalloped Potatoes and succulent carrots were like none that I'd ever tasted, and I heartily recommend them.

I was going to refuse dessert, but their friendly Scandinavian-costumed waitresses coaxed me into trying Gâteau Christina—a definite died-and-gone-to-heaven dessert.

At bedtime, my sherbet-colored bedroom suite added to the delight of finding such luxury tucked within the citrus belt. And morning breakfast began with Vita Hinshaw's invention of Broiled Grapefruit with cinnamon and sugar—perfect anywhere!

Chalet Suzanne is located off US 27, on Highway 17-A in Lake Wales. Meals are served from 8:00 a.m. until 9:30 p.m. daily. The restaurant is closed on Monday during summer months. Reservations are suggested. Call (813) 676-6011.

CHALET SUZANNE'S GATEAU CHRISTINA

Meringue:
4 egg whites
1½ cups sugar

⅓ cup blanched ground almonds

Preheat oven to 250 degrees. Cut aluminum foil into 4 8-inch circles and grease each lightly. Whip egg whites until stiff, gradually adding sugar and almonds as eggs begin to stiffen. Place foil rounds on a large baking sheet and spread each evenly with meringue. Bake for 15 minutes or until meringue is dry. Carefully turn meringues over and bake 5 minutes more.

Chocolate Filling:
2 egg whites
½ cup sugar
2 tablespoons sweetened cocoa

2 sticks butter, softened
4 ounces semisweet chocolate, melted

In the top of a double boiler, over hot (not boiling) water, beat egg whites until foamy. Gradually add sugar, cocoa, butter and chocolate, beating until thick and creamy. Remove from heat and cool.

To assemble gâteau, place the best meringue layer on the bottom and spread with chocolate. Top with another meringue, pressing down lightly to make layers fit together. Spread with chocolate. Repeat until all meringues are used and the top is liberally coated with chocolate. Cover and refrigerate for at least 24 hours. Yields 1 4-layered gateau.

NOTE: These may be stored in tin boxes for gifts.

CHALET SUZANNE'S VEAL CHOPS

1½ sticks or more butter
2 medium-sized onions, sliced
2 cups sliced fresh mushrooms
½ teaspoon celery salt
½ cup dry vermouth
salt and pepper to taste
flour for dusting

4 6- to 8-ounce veal chops
2 cups chicken broth (homemade or commercial)
1 cup or more sour cream
½ pound pasta, cooked
2 or more bananas, sliced
brown sugar to taste

Melt 2 to 3 tablespoons of the butter in a skillet and sauté onions until tender; set aside. Add 3 to 4 tablespoons of butter to the skillet and sauté mushrooms until barely tender; sprinkle them with celery salt and set aside with onions. Deglaze the skillet with a little vermouth, then pour the remaining vermouth over onions and mushrooms. Salt, pepper and lightly dust the veal with flour. Melt 4 tablespoons of butter in the skillet and brown veal on both sides. Add chicken broth to the veal; cover and bake in a 300-degree oven for about 40 minutes. Add mushrooms, onions and sour cream and bake until heated through. Serve over seasoned pasta.

In a separate skillet melt 2 or more tablespoons of butter and quickly sauté the banana slices, sprinkled with brown sugar, until brown. Arrange on plates with veal and pasta. Serves 4.

REECECLIFF
Lakeland

REECECLIFF

When one of Lakeland's home-sick residents returns after a spell away, a good cure for the homesick blues is one of Reececliff's home-baked pies. Everyone I talked with in the restaurant had a favorite pie: Apple, Cherry, Peach, Coconut Custard or Sweet Potato. But they were also agreeable to whichever pie was ready to come out of the oven. And Reececliff's may be one of the few remaining places where you can still order buttermilk or an old-fashioned malt to go with your pie. Although I was a stranger, the customers enthusiastically explained why they or their parents had been coming to this tidy little white restaurant, with its candy-stripe awning, since it opened in 1934. I was told that people come here because the owners don't take short cuts in preparing the food, and they listen to what their customers want. A recipe for success in any city.

When Reece and Clifford Stidham bought the former "Ducky Wucky" drive-in restaurant, they didn't care for the name, so the couple combined his first name with half of his wife's first name to form the name Reececliff. Periodically, the restaurant has been remodeled, and it is now being run by the family's third generation, Robert Pope. Robert insists, just as the Stidham's daughter Mildred and her husband Charlie Pope had insisted, on operating in the same tradition that his grandparents established. The dining room is clean and simple, with a kind of white-on-white décor relieved by hundreds of menus tastefully adorning the ceiling and walls. And the food is wholesome, southern-style fare.

At lunch Mrs. Pope told me that she feels the restaurant has always been a success because it serves as a kind of gathering place for people to come and exchange conversation. When waitress Jo Young, who has been with Reececliff for more than thirty years, brought me some Chicken Fried Steak, hot Banana Nut Bread and a tasty Squash Soufflé, she told me that the customers were a little nervous when they saw me taking photos of the exterior. "They're scared somebody new will come in here and change everything. It wouldn't be the same without this family." I believed her.

It would have been a sacrilege to leave without tasting one of their pies. After great deliberation, I finally chose the Cherry Pie. It was perfect, not too tart or sweet.

My lunch may sound unpretentious, just as Reececliff is, but when you taste the food, you'll know why the restaurant has lasted. While I was there, I saw a customer bring a beautiful bouquet of pink camellias to the restaurant. The incident reminded me a little of taking flowers to a friend. In fact, that's just what it was.

Reececliff is located at 940 South Florida Avenue in Lakeland. Meals are served from 9:00 a.m. until 10:00 p.m. Monday through Saturday. (The restaurant is closed the first two weeks in August.) Reservations are unnecessary, but the telephone number is (813) 686-6661.

REECECLIFF'S SQUASH SOUFFLE

2 pounds fresh yellow
  squash, chopped
1 small onion, chopped
15⅓ ounces evaporated
  milk
1 teaspoon salt
2 tablespoons melted butter
  (no substitutes)

2 eggs, beaten
2 tablespoons sugar
pepper to taste
¼ pound Cheddar cheese,
  grated
¾ cup ground potato chips
  or crackers

Steam squash and onions together until tender. Place in a bowl and add milk, salt, butter, eggs, sugar, pepper and cheese. Mix until well blended and place in a greased 8-inch-by-10-inch pan. Top with potato chips or crackers. Bake in a preheated, 325-degree oven for 45 minutes. Serves 12.

REECECLIFF'S CHERRY PIE

1 9-inch pie crust
½ cup cherry juice
1 cup sugar
¼ teaspoon salt

1 tablespoon cornstarch
1 tablespoon all-purpose
  flour
2 cups cherries, drained

Prepare a pie crust, using your favorite recipe. Make a little extra pie dough to use as strips across the top of the pie. In a bowl combine cherry juice, sugar, salt, cornstarch and flour and stir until smooth. Fold in cherries and pour this mixture into the pie crust. Take strips of dough and lace across the top in a lattice fashion, securing the ends by pressing them into the pie crust. Bake in a preheated, 325-degree oven for 45 minutes. Yields 1 pie.

REECECLIFF'S BANANA NUT BREAD

½ cup vegetable oil
1 cup sugar
2 eggs
2 cups all-purpose flour

1 teaspoon soda
½ teaspoon salt
2 large bananas, crushed
½ cup pecans (optional)

Cream oil, sugar and eggs together until smooth. Add flour gradually with soda and salt. Fold in bananas and mix until well combined. Mix in pecans, if desired. Pour into a greased and floured 1-pound loafpan and bake in a 325-degree oven for 45 minutes. Check to see if bread is done; if not, bake an additional 5 minutes or so. Yields 1 loaf.

VALENCIA GARDEN
Tampa

VALENCIA GARDEN

Salud and happy days," said Manuel Beiro every night for fifteen years as he advertised his Spanish restaurant on live television. The Valencia Garden ad, which may hold the record as the world's longest continuously running live television commercial, is still remembered by Tampa residents who have long forgotten the "Shock Theater" shows it sponsored.

Manuel Beiro opened his Valencia Garden restaurant in Tampa in 1927. Born in Spain, near Santiago de Compostela, he decorated his restaurant with murals of his beloved homeland, painted by noted artist Harry Bierce. The mayor of Seville personally sent him the tiles used below the artwork. The restaurant's equally authentic Spanish food attracted a faithful following in Tampa's Hispanic community.

David Agliano, the founder's grandson, now manages a greatly expanded Valencia Garden. He recalls with fondness his grandparents, who lived upstairs in the house behind the restaurant. "My grandmother Rose did everything around here," he said. "She called the restaurant her 'little house' and would put out flowers and sweep the parking lot. The two of them worked seven days a week, every day of the year. My grandmother was always one to make you laugh. The restaurant was like a warm and inviting home."

Though the restaurant now seats three hundred in numerous rooms, David Agliano still tries to preserve that personal touch. He has no maître d' at lunch, but seats everyone himself, talking with regulars who have come to Valencia Garden for years for traditional "Tampa Spanish" food.

The menu includes such favorites as Arroz con Pollo, Paella, Cuban Black Bean Soup, Ropa Vieja (shredded beef with onions and tomatoes) and Papillot (fish stuffed with shrimp and lobster and baked in french paper). I began my lunch with Caldo Gallego, a hearty soup made with ham hocks and turnip greens—a treat for a southern girl like me. The Shrimp Ajillo that followed was delicious, as was the Cuban bread.

My waiter, employed at Valencia Garden since 1953 (he served the food on that television ad!), was eager for me to try their Crema Española. David Agliano told me that his restaurant is one of the very few to offer this difficult-to-perfect dessert. So I took "just one more bite" and was glad I did. It was superb.—B.R.M.

Valencia Garden is located at 811 West John F. Kennedy Boulevard in Tampa. Lunch is served Monday through Friday from 11:00 a.m. to 2:30 p.m.; dinner is served Monday through Saturday from 5:00 p.m. to 10:00 p.m. For reservations (not required), call (813) 253-3773.

VALENCIA GARDEN'S CREMA ESPANOLA

1 cup light cream
¼ cup flour
1 cup sugar
1½ teaspoons vanilla

3 cups milk
8 egg yolks
1 tablespoon butter

Topping:
1 teaspoon cinnamon
½ cup sugar

Mix cream, flour, sugar and vanilla in a mixing bowl with a hand beater. Meanwhile, bring milk to a boil. Add hot milk to cream mixture and beat with a hand mixer until smooth. Cook the mixture in the top pot of a double boiler until thickened. In a mixing bowl beat egg yolks until smooth. Then pour hot mixture into eggs, stirring rapidly. Return mixture to double boiler and add butter. Cook 25 to 35 minutes, stirring frequently. Pour mixture into a 1½-quart glass serving dish. Cool.

Combine ½ cup sugar and the cinnamon. Sprinkle mixture on top of cooled cream. (For burnt or caramelized topping at home, you can place the dish under the broiler until topping is brown.) Refrigerate. Serves 6.

VALENCIA GARDEN'S CALDO GALLEGO

1 1½-pound ham hock
½-pound lean beef
½-pound salt pork
1 bunch turnip greens
dash of nutmeg
1 cup Great Northern white
   beans, soaked
1 onion, chopped

1 green pepper, chopped
1 garlic clove, minced
3 tablespoons bacon grease
3 potatoes, peeled and
   cubed
2 chorizos
salt to taste

In a 4-quart pot, place ham hock, beef and pork. Cover with water and bring to a boil. Skim several times. Cook over medium heat until tender, about 1 hour. Chop greens and add to meat. Add nutmeg and beans (drained). Cook uncovered at low heat for 30 minutes. In a skillet, sauté onions, green peppers and garlic in bacon grease. Add to soup. Add potatoes and chorizos, and salt to taste. Cover and cook 45 minutes longer, until potatoes are done. Serves 6.

THE COLUMBIA
Tampa

THE COLUMBIA

The Columbia, in Tampa's historic Ybor City, combines robust Spanish food, dramatic architecture, traditional Latin entertainment and Old World courtliness to create a cultural adventure not to be missed. Proudly proclaimed the oldest restaurant in Florida and the oldest and largest Spanish restaurant in the United States, the Columbia has been in the same family for four generations.

The present-day Columbia covers an entire city block. It has eleven rooms, with a seating capacity of 1,660. It also has its own commissary, coffee mill and laundry.

It all began in 1905 when Casimiro Hernandez, Sr., a Cuban immigrant, opened a coffee shop and bar. Tampa's cigar industry was in its heyday in Ybor City then, and the thousands of Spanish-speaking residents outnumbered the English-speaking population. The cafe soon became a favorite of locals, and a new dining room had to be added in 1920.

After the death of the older Hernandez in 1929, his son Casimiro Hernandez, Jr., took over the management. Under his direction, in 1935 the Columbia became the first restaurant in Florida to be air-conditioned. In 1936 Hernandez built the richly ornate Don Quixote Dining Room with its splendid Bacarat crystal chandelier. The next year he added more rooms and a two-story, glass-roofed interior courtyard, complete with a balcony and a sculptured fountain which is a focal point of the restaurant today.

A great admirer of the famous Spanish writer Cervantes, Hernandez commissioned a Tampa artist, Sergio de Meza, to paint scenes from *Don Quixote*. Every day for thirty years the artist ate three meals a day at the Columbia, producing seventy-nine paintings of Don Quixote, as well as impressive copies of old masters. Many of these paintings hang on the walls of the vast restaurant today.

Cesar Gonzmart, married to Hernandez's only child, Adela, entered the family business in 1953 and expanded the restaurant even more. Branches were opened in Sarasota in 1959 and in St. Augustine in 1983; they are run by sons Casey and Richard.

Tall and distinguished, Gonzmart personally greets guests throughout his restaurant. An accomplished musician who once served as concertmaster of the Havana Symphony, he still thrills audiences with occasional violin performances at the Columbia.

Numerous customers have come weekly, even daily, for years to enjoy traditional Spanish favorites like Cuban Black Bean Soup, Chilled Gazpacho, Chicken and Yellow Rice "Ybor," Cuban-style steak and Snapper Alicante.

More than fifteen hundred articles have been written about the Columbia in its more than eighty years of existence. For many, it is the symbol of the city of Tampa. The night I visited, a French television station was filming the flamenco dancers for a documentary on Tampa. The castanets, pounding feet and swirling skirts, the delicious sangria and the warmth and drama of the décor made for a perfect television clip, and for a perfect evening.—B.R.M.

The Columbia is located at 2117 East Seventh Avenue in Tampa's Ybor City historic district. It is open daily for lunch and dinner, from 11:00 a.m. to 11:00 p.m. On Sunday, a Cuban feast begins at noon. For reservations, call (813) 248-4961.

THE COLUMBIA'S SNAPPER ALICANTE

2½-pound snapper fillets
1 onion, cut in round slices
2 green peppers, cut in
   rings
12 almonds
¼ cup olive oil
½ teaspoon salt

pinch of white pepper
½ cup brown gravy
½ cup white wine
Shrimp Supreme (recipe
   below)
4 slices breaded eggplant

NOTE: Before you begin preparing the snapper, marinate the shrimp for the Shrimp Supreme (see instructions below).

In a casserole (preferably clay) place snapper fillets on top of onion slices. Top with pepper rings and almonds. Pour the olive oil, salt, pepper, brown gravy and wine over fish. Bake uncovered at 350 degrees for 25 minutes. Meanwhile, prepare the Shrimp Supreme and fry the eggplant. Garnish baked snapper with shrimp and eggplant. Serves 2.

Shrimp Supreme:

4 large shrimp, shelled	**1 egg**
¼ cup lemon juice	**¼ cup milk**
salt and pepper to taste	**½ cup flour**
2 strips bacon, cut in half	**fat or oil for frying**

Marinate the shrimp in lemon juice, salt and pepper for 1 hour. Wrap marinated shrimp with a half slice of bacon each; skewer bacon in place with a toothpick. Mix egg and milk into a batter. Dip shrimp in batter, then roll in flour. Deep-fry in fat until golden brown.

THE COLUMBIA'S CHICKEN AND YELLOW RICE "YBOR"

1 3-pound chicken	**2 cups long-grain rice**
½ cup olive oil	**1 bay leaf**
2 onions, chopped	**1 tablespoon salt (or less if**
1 green pepper, chopped	**desired)**
2 medium-sized tomatoes,	**¼ cup white wine**
peeled, seeded and	**½ cup small green peas**
chopped	**(frozen or canned)**
2 cloves garlic, minced	**2 pimientos, cut in half**
4 cups chicken broth	**4 asparagus tips**
½ teaspoon saffron	

Cut the fryer into quarters. In a skillet, sauté chicken in heated olive oil until the skin is golden. Remove chicken and place in a casserole. In the same oil sauté onions, green peppers, tomatoes and garlic for 5 minutes. Pour over chicken; then add chicken broth, saffron, rice, bay leaf and salt to the skillet. When it begins to boil, pour mixture over the other ingredients in the casserole. Cover casserole and bake in a 350-degree oven for 20 minutes. Take the dish out of the oven, sprinkle it with wine and garnish with peas, pimientos and asparagus tips. Serves 4.

KACIN'S CASABLANCA CAFE
Tampa

KACIN'S CASABLANCA CAFE

The Moorish arches hint of intrigue at Kacin's Casablanca Cafe, located in the hotel where Humphrey Bogart stayed while filming *Key Largo*. The hotel, now awaiting restoration, was built in the 1920s by Tampa's colorful developer, David P. Davis.

Inspired by Miami Beach's Carl Fisher and Coral Gables's George Merrick, Davis bought up two marshy, partially submerged islands, Big Grassy and Little Grassy, and dredged and filled them to create Davis Islands in 1925. Marketed as the "eighth wonder of the world," his Mediterranean development provided some of the most striking architecture in Tampa. In addition to the hotel, the island complex had fine residences, a hospital, baseball diamond, tennis courts, marina, park, golf course and airport.

Eleven years ago, Bob Kacin, an avid sailor, was captivated by the old hotel, which is located near the marina he used. He convinced his wife to open a restaurant in what was the hotel's courtyard, where tea dances had been held in its better years. Though they have since enclosed their restaurant, the exotic, tropical flavor of the atmosphere and the personally prepared food have kept customers coming ever since.

Barbara Kacin is one of those incredible people who can never get enough of cooking. She prepares many of the dishes herself at the restaurant, and then she cooks to relax at home, experimenting with new concoctions all the time. The results show in her restaurant.

The Casablanca's seafood is renowned, with only fresh ingredients used in such specialties as Moroccan Grouper (sautéed with macadamia nuts and flamed in wine) and Maryland Crab Cakes.

Their ever-changing homemade desserts also draw people like magnets. In fact, the Kacins did a survey once in their restaurant and found that they averaged one dessert per customer. "If someone doesn't eat a dessert here," Bob Kacin remarked, "then someone else must be eating two."

I was in that second group. The special dessert of the day, Apple Cobbler, was the best I've ever eaten. And I just couldn't resist the Sky High Ice Cream Pie. The caloric intake was sky high, but so was the enjoyment.—B.R.M.

Kacin's Casablanca Cafe is located at 115 East Davis Boulevard on Davis Islands in Tampa. Lunch is served Monday through Friday from 11:45 a.m. to 2:30 p.m.; dinner is served Monday through Thursday from 6:00 to 10:00 p.m., and on Friday and Saturday from 6:00 to 10:30 p.m. For reservations call (813) 251-9770.

KACIN'S CASABLANCA CAFE'S SEAFOOD JAMBALAYA

1 pound boneless chicken
½ pound chorizo sausage
½ pound smoked ham, trimmed
½ pound medium shrimp
1 medium onion
1 medium green pepper
2 tablespoons parsley
3 medium celery ribs
3 large garlic cloves
8 ounces lump crabmeat
12 large shrimp
1 to 2 tablespoons chicken fat (or butter)

1 28-ounce can peeled tomatoes, with juice
2 cups chicken stock
3 crushed bay leaves
1 teaspoon Tabasco sauce (more if you like it hotter)
2 teaspoons Cajun seasoning
3 tablespoons Worcestershire sauce
½ teaspoon paprika
1 teaspoon salt
1 cup rice

Cut chicken, sausage and ham into 1-inch cubes. Shell and devein the medium shrimp and cut it into pieces. Chop the onion, pepper, parsley and celery, and mince the garlic. Pick the crabmeat from shells; peel, devein and butterfly the large shrimp. Set aside.

Melt butter or fat in a large pot over moderate heat. Add chicken and stir rapidly for 1 minute. Add chorizo sausage and ham and cook for 1 minute. Add ½ pound shrimp and the chopped vegetables and cook for another minute. Next, add tomatoes, chicken stock, bay leaves, Tabasco, Cajun seasoning, Worcestershire sauce, paprika and salt. Add rice; cover and cook until rice is done, stirring occasionally. Before serving, add crabmeat and 1 dozen shrimp, cooking just until shrimp is done (pink and slightly curled). Serves 8.

KACIN'S CASABLANCA CAFE'S BASIC
VANILLA ICE CREAM

1 quart whipping cream
1 vanilla bean, split in half
dash of salt

¾ cup sugar
2 egg yolks
1 teaspoon vanilla extract

In the top of a double boiler, add whipping cream, vanilla bean, salt and sugar. Bring water to a boil; heat the cream mixture until a skin forms on top. Remove from heat and allow cream to cool slightly. Add egg yolks, stirring rapidly. Strain into an ice-cream can. With a sharp knife, scrape seeds from vanilla pods and add seeds to cream mixture. Add vanilla extract. Chill ice-cream mixture overnight. Make ice cream according to manufacturer's instructions. Yields 1 quart.

KACIN'S CASABLANCA CAFE'S
SKY HIGH ICE CREAM PIE

12 to 20 chocolate chip
  cookies
1 pint coffee ice cream
1 pint vanilla ice cream

1 pint butter pecan ice
  cream (or macadamia
  nut)
2 cups chocolate sauce

Line the bottom of a 9- or 10-inch springform pan with your favorite chocolate chip cookies. (Depending on the size of the cookies, it may take more or less than the number listed above.) Fill the inside of the pie with softened commercial or homemade ice cream in layers of different flavors. Top with chocolate sauce. Freeze until ready to serve. Serves 8 to 10.

SIPLE'S GARDEN SEAT
Clearwater

SIPLE'S GARDEN SEAT Three hundred and ninety-two years before Mary Boardman left Maine for Clearwater, Panfilo de Narvaez maneuvered his fleet into Clearwater Harbor. It is thought, though not proven, that Panfilo brought his six hundred men (Clearwater's first tourists) to the very spot where Boardman later established Siple's Garden Seat. The fishing opportunities and spectacular view make this a natural conclusion. After all, the area is what enticed Boardman to purchase Nanny Boyd's turn-of-the-century board-and-batten "cracker" home around 1920 and turn it into a fashionable tea room.

Back in the twenties, when tea rooms were in their heyday, ladies bedecked in flowered hats sipped tea and nibbled little sandwiches and pastries in the garden here, while their less fortunate chauffeurs gathered around tables in the kitchen. Soon, though, lunch and dinner gained ground as Boardman became famous for beef, imported in barrels, and a special recipe for Strawberry Ice Cream that was always served at Thanksgiving. After the winter season, family and staff packed up and moved to their Adirondacks restaurant for the summer season. That, of course, is a page from the past now that Clearwater has become a year-round vacation land.

From my table in the Veranda Dining Room, I could see a fisherman pulling in his net as I was served a brunch special called Salmon Egg. What an innovative idea to have potato pancakes covered with Norwegian salmon and a poached egg and laced with hollandaise. It seems that the restaurant's third generation is continuing their grandmother's tradition of serving unusual combinations of first-class foods.

My favorite brunch entrées were Chicken with Athenian Sauce and Curry of Seafood Chad Richard. I later learned that the sauces in these dishes are "go with anything" sauces— good with scallops, shrimp or grouper. They certainly went well with my glass of Chardonnay. Sometimes Siple's offers their unusual International Meatballs with Vodka for brunch, a dish my family would devour at *any* meal.

Everybody's heard of Pecan Pie, but have you ever heard of or tasted Royal Macadamia Nut Pie? Theirs is a kissing cousin to pecan, but better than any pecan pie I've eaten.

You can't come here to eat without being affected by your surroundings. But the owners only take credit for the food, as I discovered when I tried to compliment them on their waterfront garden setting. "The Lord is the landscape architect. We just take care of it." And good caretakers they are.

Siple's Garden Seat is located at 1234 Druid Road South in Clearwater. Lunch is served from 11:30 a.m. until 3:00 p.m., and dinner is served from 6:00 p.m. until 9:30 p.m. Monday through Friday, and from 5:30 p.m. until 10:00 p.m. on Saturday. Sunday brunch is served from 11:30 a.m. until 3:00 p.m., and dinner until 8:30 p.m. Reservations are not mandatory but are requested. Call (813) 44SIPLE.

SIPLE'S GARDEN SEAT'S CHICKEN WITH ATHENIAN SAUCE

Athenian Sauce:

½ **cup olive oil**
2 **ounces clarified butter**
1¼ **teaspoons oregano**
1¼ **teaspoons minced garlic**

juice of half a lemon
¾ **cup feta cheese,**
    crumbled

Mix all ingredients together in a stainless steel bowl. Make sure that the cheese is finely crumbled. Cover and refrigerate.

Chicken:

4 **deboned chicken breasts,**
    skinned
flour for dusting
salt and pepper to taste

3 **tablespoons olive oil**
½ **cup sliced fresh**
    mushrooms
½ **cup chopped onions**

Pound chicken breasts with a mallet to an even thickness. Dust with flour seasoned with salt and pepper; cover and refrigerate for a few minutes. Heat olive oil in a skillet and sauté chicken breasts with mushrooms and onions until lightly done. Add 2 ounces of sauce to each chicken breast and bake in a 450-degree oven for 2 to 3 minutes. Serves 4.

SIPLE'S GARDEN SEAT'S CURRY OF SEAFOOD CHAD RICHARD

1 quart mayonnaise
1 cup chutney
1 tablespoon lemon juice
1 tablespoon curry

8 ounces fettucine
6 shrimp, cooked
6 scallops, steamed
6 langostini

Mix mayonnaise and chutney together. Add lemon juice and curry and blend well. Refrigerate sauce. Prepare fettucine according to package directions. In a greased, ovenproof dish combine the fish with fettucine and stir in 12 ounces of the sauce until well combined. (Leftover sauce can be stored in the refrigerator and used on any fish.) Bake in a preheated 350-degree oven for 8 to 10 minutes. Serves 4.

SIPLE'S GARDEN SEAT'S INTERNATIONAL MEATBALLS IN VODKA

2½ pounds hamburger
2 eggs
2 cups cracker crumbs
½ pound ground lean pork
½ teaspoon lemon rind, grated
¼ teaspoon nutmeg
1 teaspoon salt
¼ teaspoon pepper
1 cup milk

3 to 4 tablespoons bacon drippings or butter
3 cups thinly sliced onions
1 cup sour cream
2 tablespoons flour
1 cup condensed beef bouillon
1 ounce dry vermouth
1 ounce vodka

Mix the first 9 ingredients together in a large bowl; cover and refrigerate for 1 hour. Remove and shape into small meatballs. Heat drippings or butter in a skillet and cook meatballs and onions together over medium-low heat for about 15 minutes or until done. Remove from pan. Add sour cream to pan and stir in flour to thicken. Add beef bouillon and stir until blended. Place meatballs and onions back in the pan, then stir in vermouth and vodka and heat through. Serves 8 to 10.

BELLEVIEW BILTMORE
Clearwater

BELLEVIEW BILTMORE The trunks started arriving in Clearwater in January and weren't packed again until April, when their wealthy owners returned to their own homes scattered across the country. That was in 1897, twelve years after Dr. Van Bibber's paper to the American Medical Association declared this to be the optimum place for a health city.

Shortly after the "discovery" of Clearwater, Henry Plant purchased the local railroad and constructed his rambling white-frame, green-gabled Belleview, which is said still to be the largest occupied wooden structure in the world. The Biltmore chain bought the hotel in the '30s and changed its name to the Belleview Biltmore.

Spanish explorer Hernando de Soto came to this region looking for gold, but found instead five mineral springs which he named Esperitu Santo or "Springs of Sacred Spirit" because the Tocobaga Indians at the large nearby village believed the springs had healing powers. Perhaps that is one reason the Belleview Biltmore included hot mineral baths in their magnificent new European-styled spa. Unfortunately, I was there a week shy of opening, so I can't attest to the spa's many benefits, but I can attest to the splendor of staying in one of the most luxuriously refurbished Victorian hotels in the country—and to enjoying a tantalizing mixture of regional and continental food.

After a revitalizing round of golf on the same course that prompted the Duke of Windsor to become the hotel's best unofficial public relations enthusiast, I entered the Tiffany Dining Room. My eyes were immediately drawn to the original barrel-vaulted stained-glass ceiling panels. Only then did they drift to double columns, banked with palms, flowing through the center of this elegant room.

My friends and I began by sampling three quite unusual soups. The first was a beef-flavored Jellied Soup, next their lovely, light Cantaloupe Supreme, and finally a richer Avocado Soup Carmel. Perhaps I'm not always accurate, but I often can tell a lot about a restaurant just by tasting its house

110

dressing. The Belleview's is more than worthy of our recipe section. For my entrée, I chose an old favorite—Veal Oscar. Their chef includes crabmeat in his version of this classic, and I wasn't disappointed.

Desserts change each day here, and some are especially designed for the health spa dieters, as are some of their entrées and other dishes. We decided on coffee and a moonlit stroll on the beach overlooking the Gulf of Mexico.

The Belleview Biltmore is located at 25 Belleview Boulevard in Clearwater. Meals are served daily. Breakfast is served from 7:30 a.m. until 10:00 p.m.; lunch is served from noon until 2:00 p.m.; and dinner is served from 6:00 p.m. until 9:00 p.m. For reservations (suggested) call (813) 442-6171. For toll-free calls, dial 1-800-237-8947.

BELLEVIEW BILTMORE'S CANTALOUPE SUPREME

4 cups cubed cantaloupe, chilled (or casaba or Persian melon)
⅔ cup lemon juice, chilled
salt and pepper to taste
⅓ cup cognac
½ teaspoon minced fresh ginger

Place all ingredients in a blender or food processor and blend until liquid and foamy. Serve with an ice cube in each bowl. Serves 4.

BELLEVIEW BILTMORE'S HOUSE DRESSING

1 tablespoon fresh Parmesan cheese, grated
½ tablespoon ground black pepper
½ large garlic clove, minced
pinch of monosodium glutamate (optional)
½ tablespoon fresh lemon juice
½ tablespoon onion juice
dash of Tabasco sauce
½ tablespoon Worcestershire sauce
½ tablespoon cider vinegar
1 cup mayonnaise
2 ounces buttermilk
salt to taste

Mix the first 9 ingredients together in a blender or food processor until well mixed. Add mayonnaise, buttermilk and salt, blending until smooth. Yields 1 pint.

111

BELLEVIEW BILTMORE'S VEAL OSCAR

4 4-ounce veal cutlets
¾ cup all-purpose flour
salt and pepper to taste
1 egg
2 tablespoons milk
½ stick butter

12 asparagus spears,
   steamed
8 pieces crabmeat (leg, if
   possible)
Béarnaise Sauce (recipe
   below)

Pound veal until very thin. Dredge in flour seasoned with salt and pepper. Whip egg and milk together and dip veal in egg wash mixture. Melt butter in a skillet and sauté veal until golden brown on both sides. Place veal on warmed plates and top each with 3 asparagus spears and 2 pieces crabmeat. Ladle Béarnaise over top. Serves 4.

Béarnaise Sauce:
4 tablespoons fresh tar-
   ragon, chopped
6 tablespoons fresh chervil
1 teaspoon chopped
   scallions
1 teaspoon pepper

pinch of salt
4 tablespoons red wine
   vinegar
5 egg yolks
¾ cup melted butter
cayenne pepper to taste

Reserve a teaspoon each of tarragon and chervil. Put the remaining tarragon and chervil in a saucepan with the scallions, pepper, salt and vinegar. Simmer over medium heat until vinegar is reduced by two-thirds. Remove from heat, and let pan cool to warm stage. Add egg yolks, stirring into a paste. Return pan to very low heat and stir in melted butter until well combined. Remove from heat and strain the mixture through a sieve and finish with a teaspoon each of chopped chervil and tarragon. Sprinkle with cayenne to taste.

NOTE: Use only half the amount of spices listed when using dried spices.

THE KING CHARLES
IN THE DON CESAR
St. Petersburg Beach

THE KING CHARLES IN THE DON CESAR BEACH RESORT

The pink spires and barrel-tile roof of the majestic Don CeSar Beach Resort can be seen for miles, a rosy-hued beacon by land or by sea. Looking at the imposing beauty of this tribute to romanticism and perseverance, it's hard to imagine that less than twenty years ago there were people who wanted to destroy it, to tear it down for a public park.

This lack of vision wouldn't have surprised the man who built the Don CeSar in the first place, back around 1925. Against the advice of everyone, Thomas J. Rowe, who moved from Virginia to Florida for health reasons, purchased a desolate eighty-acre tract of land on the inaccessible island of Pass-a-Grille, near St. Petersburg.

Inspired by the architecture of George Merrick's Coral Gables, James Deering's Vizcaya and Addison Mizner's Palm Beach and Boca Raton, Rowe turned the wilderness into a subdivision of Mediterranean-style homes. For the crowning glory of his development, he lavished $1,250,000 on a magnificent hotel. He named it the Don CeSar after Don Caesar, the leading character in his favorite American opera, *Maritana*.

The hotel was built on shifting beach sand by using a floating pad of concrete and pyramided footings so thick and strong that they have yet to show any signs of settling.

After a glorious gala opening January 16, 1928, and a few prosperous years, during which it was only open for "the season" of January and February, the Great Depression took its toll. Famous patrons such as F. Scott Fitzgerald and his wife Zelda, novelist Faith Baldwin, attorney Clarence Darrow and the entire New York Yankees baseball team came and went.

The army took over the hotel in 1942 as a hospital. It became the Air Force Convalescent Center in 1944, then the Veterans Administration Regional Office. With each change, more and more of the once-luxurious interior was stripped and institutionalized. Its appearance deteriorated and in 1969 the building was abandoned, left to vandals and pigeons.

Amid cries of "tear the eyesore down," writer June Hurley Young started to publicize its plight. In 1971 hotelier William

Bowman, Jr., accepted the challenge of restoring the Don CeSar to its original opulence, a job that required twelve thousand gallons of flamingo pink paint and the removal and replacement, pane by pane, of thirteen thousand pieces of glass to refinish the original windows.

The second gala opening of the Don CeSar was held November 24, 1973, to the delight of the community. The hotel is now owned by CIGNA, and $8 million more was spent in 1986 to further modernize the interior.

The King Charles is on the fifth floor, overlooking the Gulf of Mexico. The high ceilings, French windows, crystal chandeliers, and seafoam-and-pink décor bespeak refined elegance, a fitting atmosphere for the French cuisine served.

Menu selections are carefully designed to make each offering beautiful to the eye as well as the taste. All the ingredients are fresh; all artistically presented. Their $50,000 wine cellar and their ever-changing selections of seafood, lamb, veal, beef, duck and chicken dishes have won them many culinary awards. The Salade de Homard I was served was, quite simply, unforgettable perfection.—B.R.M.

The King Charles is located in the Don CeSar Beach Resort at 3400 Gulf Boulevard in St. Petersburg Beach. Dinner only is served Monday through Saturday, from 6:00 to 10:00 p.m. Brunch is served on Sunday from 10:30 a.m. to 2:30 p.m. Gentlemen are required to wear dinner jackets. Reservations are recommended; phone (813) 360-1881.

THE KING CHARLES' MEDAILLONS
DE VEAU QUIBERON

3 fresh asparagus spears
2 baby carrots
2 baby yellow squash
2 baby potatoes
2 tablespoons butter
6 ounces veal tenderloin, cut in small pieces

6 ounces lobster medallions, sliced from poached lobster tail
1 tablespoon Beluga caviar
2 to 3 tablespoons Béarnaise Sauce (see Index)
4 or 5 fresh tarragon leaves

115

Cook whole vegetables in boiling water for 3 to 4 minutes; drain and sauté a minute or so in half the butter. In a different pan, sauté veal in the remaining tablespoon of butter. Remove veal from pan. Add poached lobster medallions to the pan and quickly warm. Arrange veal and lobster on a plate and top with caviar and Béarnaise Sauce. Arrange vegetables attractively around the meat and garnish with tarragon leaves. Serves 1.

THE KING CHARLES' SALADE DE HOMARD AUX TRUFFLES ET CAVIAR

1 1½-pound Maine lobster, poached and chilled
Salad Dressing (recipe below)
1 head of endive
1 large tomato, quartered
1 artichoke heart, quartered
½ avocado, peeled and sliced

4 asparagus spears, crisply cooked
1 piece heart of palm, cut in chunks
1 tablespoon Beluga caviar
½ truffle, chopped (canned)
¼ head radicchio
1 edible violet flower

Pull meat off poached and chilled lobster. Toss the meat together with Salad Dressing and all ingredients except the violet. Arrange artistically on a large plate and top with a violet. Serves 1.

THE KING CHARLES' SALAD DRESSING

1 cup olive oil
¼ cup wine vinegar
1 teaspoon Dijon mustard

1 teaspoon salt
1 teaspoon pepper
squeeze of lemon juice

Mix all ingredients until well blended. Pour over salad. Yields 1¼ cups.

COLEY'S
Sarasota

COLEY'S

When George Prime built his hardware store in downtown Sarasota in 1915, I'm sure he never dreamed that it would one day be Sarasota's hangout for the theater crowd. But after Prohibition, the hardware store was converted into a bar called the Circus Bar. In other regions of the country the word *circus* might have various connotations, but in Sarasota, the winter quarters of the Ringling Brothers Circus, it had only one.

John Ringling and his wife Mable moved here in 1890 and built their famed winter estate, a combination of architectural styles ranging from neo-Gothic Venetian to Italian Renaissance. Ringling also built a hotel called the Ringling Towers for his circus stars. The hotel is gone, but Ringling's stunning estate, now an immense art museum, is worth a visit. It houses what is considered one of the finest Baroque art collection in America. You can also see Ringling's *Ca 'd' Zan* (house of John), with its fresco ceilings, marble baths and other remarkable signatures of that opulent age. People of all ages, whether circus buffs or not, will also enjoy the circus museum, erected in 1948 to hold circus art and memorabilia.

I expect that many of Ringling's performers frequented the Circus Bar, just as these days local theater actors and audiences hang out at Coley's before and after shows. The restaurant has several sections, each with a different personality. In the front room, skylights with lots of flowing greenery make this a bright and airy place for lunch, or you may prefer a seat at the bar, where you can view all the liquor stored in the old oak dairy bar. The mounted deer's head above the bar will no doubt be wearing the hat of the season, or perhaps one from a current theatrical production. The bar and back room both have a pressed-tin ceiling brought from a bar in Rochester, New York, and the back room, with its exposed brick walls, is decorated with old portraits in heavy gilt frames and with hanging Tiffany lamps.

I sat at a booth in the back room and people-watched as I sampled their crunchy Beer Batter Fried Zucchini, an imported beer and a fresh Green Salad mixed with their multipurpose Dill Dressing. I tried a bit of the dressing on Chicken Wings, Potato Skins and even Char-broiled Shrimp. The taste varies but works with each one. Then it was time for some of their "not too spicy" Chili, which was made with lots of meat and served with some terrific French garlic bread. For me, lunch is a bit too early for Spanish Coffee, but next time, say after a play, I'll try this intriguing concoction.

Coley's is located at 1355 Main Street in Sarasota. Meals are served from 11:30 a.m. until 2:00 a.m Monday through Friday. Saturday and Sunday meals are served from 5:00 p.m. until 2:00 a.m. Reservations are suggested. Call (813) 955-5627.

COLEY'S CHILI

2 to 3 tablespoons butter
1 pound ground chuck
2 green peppers, seeded
  and diced
1 large Spanish onion,
  diced
¼ teaspoon garlic salt
½ teaspoon chili powder

pinch of cayenne pepper
1 16-ounce can whole
  tomatoes in juice
1 16-ounce can crushed
  tomatoes
1 16-ounce can red kidney
  beans

In a large Dutch oven, melt butter and brown the meat with peppers and onions until vegetables are tender. Drain grease from pan. Add garlic salt, chili powder and cayenne pepper, stirring until well mixed. Add cans of tomatoes and kidney beans and stir until mixed together. Lower heat to medium-low and cook for about an hour and a half, stirring frequently. Taste and adjust seasonings if desired. Serves 8.

COLEY'S BEER BATTER FRIED ZUCCHINI

2 large zucchini
2 cups self-rising flour
5 tablespoons butter,
  melted
2 eggs
8 ounces regular domestic
  beer

pinch of salt
pinch of white pepper
pinch of garlic salt
4 drops lemon juice
oil for deep-frying

Wash zucchini and slice ¼-inch thick on the diagonal; cover and set aside. In an electric mixer, mix flour with butter and eggs. Add beer, mixing until combined. Add spices and lemon juice and mix for about 10 minutes. Heat oil in a deep-fryer until hot. Hand-dip zucchini in batter and deep-fry in oil for about 3 to 5 minutes until it turns golden brown. Serves 4.

CABBAGE KEY INN AND RESTAURANT
Bokeelia

CABBAGE KEY INN AND RESTAURANT

The thing to do on Cabbage Key is nothing, but you'll learn to do it well. You'll even flirt with the idea of chucking civilization altogether. Since you can only get here by boat, and there are no telephones or television sets, you relearn socialization. Here the people you meet are the amenities.

It was, no doubt, the isolation that convinced famed mystery writer, Mary Roberts Rinehart, and her family to build a home here in the 1930s, high above an Indian shell mound. Decades ahead of her time, Rinehart put a solar heating system on the roof of this enduring Bermuda-style home.

In the thirties you might have run into Rinehart's fishing buddy, Ernest Hemingway. The best tarpon in the Intracoastal Waterway lured him and the often reclusive Rinehart to fish here daily. If you aren't a "do nothinger" like me, it's still the place for tarpon and sailing.

The view from my pine-paneled bedroom showed the purple-blue iridescent waters where, during the boat trip, I had watched dolphins frolic as endangered species of birds soared and dipped overhead. After dropping my luggage, I settled in at the bar and was introduced to a Cabbage Creeper. One will take the edge off a travel-weary soul, but too many creepers could whittle you down to something with the mental capacity of the plant in the drink's name.

It was near sunset, so owner Rob Wells took me for an island tour, explaining that most of the dense primeval vegetation has been here since the Calusa Indians inhabited the islands. Archeological finds from the shell mounds date man's existence here from 145 B.C. The once dominant Calusa tribe, known for their highly developed art, also engaged in ritualistic human sacrifice around 1200 A.D., normally with captives taken in battle. But attack from the Spanish and northern Indians dissolved the tribe, except for a few who found their way to the Everglades and Cuba.

You can change for dinner if you like, but your comfort is what matters. In the back dining room, which gives the feel of being cantilevered in the jungle, I sat at a long table beside one

122

of the last Calusas, deck master Terry Forge. Our appetizer of Char-broil Shrimp, prepared with Sanibel Pinks, was without equal, which is probably why we ate them so fast.

I had a terrific Sautéed Grouper, then other guests shared their Stone Crab Claws with me. This dish just may be the restaurant's best. But any shrimp devotee is going to be pleased with the Spatatini Noodles with Sanibel Pinks. The dish has a fresh lemony trace to enhance it. And you must never go to Cabbage Key without having their frozen Key Lime Pie. Freezing is the catalyst for its superb taste.

The next morning, winding down the conch shell-lined walk to the dock, I realized that when you spend time here, you are revitalized by doing nothing but absorbing the peace and tropical beauty of this very special place. One night here isn't enough; you'll want more.

Cabbage Key Inn and Restaurant is located off Bokeelia. Breakfast is served from 7:30 a.m. until 9:00 a.m. Monday through Saturday, and until 10:00 a.m. on Sunday. Lunch is served from 11:30 a.m. until 3:00 p.m. Monday through Friday, and until 4:00 p.m. on Saturday, and 6:00 p.m. on Sunday. Dinner is served from 7:00 p.m. until 9:00 p.m. Monday through Saturday. To arrange transportation and reservations, call (813) 283-2278.

CABBAGE KEY'S CHAR-BROIL SHRIMP

3 sticks margarine
3 sticks butter
¼ cup sherry
¼ cup lemon juice
4 ounces fresh garlic,
    puréed

pinch of thyme
pinch of oregano
3 pounds shrimp, peeled
    and deveined

Melt margarine and butter on low heat. Add sherry, lemon juice, garlic, thyme and oregano. Remove pan from heat and let cool to room temperature. Add shrimp to the pan and let them marinate about 1 hour. Sauté shrimp until half-done

123

(about a minute). Finish shrimp over the open flame of an outside barbecue grill. Serve with melted butter. Serves 8 to 10.

CABBAGE KEY'S CHICKEN

4 boneless chicken breasts
salt to taste
white pepper to taste
flour for dusting
3 tablespoons lemon butter
(see Index for Key Lime
   Butter)

18 to 20 fresh mushrooms,
   sliced
4 sprigs parsley, chopped
4 ounces white wine
½ pound cooked rice or
   noodles

Flatten chicken to an even thickness by tapping it with a mallet. Lightly salt and pepper both sides. Dust lightly with flour. Make Key Lime Butter by substituting lime juice. Heat half of this butter in a skillet and sauté chicken on both sides. Place chicken on warm plates. Add remaining butter to the skillet and sauté mushrooms with parsley. Stir in white wine and let the sauce reduce on low heat until it begins to thicken. Pour sauce over chicken and serve with rice or noodles. Serves 4.

CABBAGE KEY'S HOUSE DRESSING

1 teaspoon Dijon mustard
1 teaspoon horseradish
¾ cup red wine vinegar
¼ cup vegetable oil

salt and pepper to taste
2 tablespoons blue cheese,
   crumbled

Whisk together mustard and horseradish. Gradually add vinegar, and without stopping, slowly add oil. Whisk vigorously until smooth. Salt and pepper to taste, then whisk in the cheese. Yields 1 cup.

KING'S CROWN DINING ROOM
Captiva Island

KING'S CROWN DINING ROOM

Long before Ponce de Leon dropped anchor in San Carlos Bay in 1513, Captiva was the site of Indian settlements. Though Captiva and Sanibel together were known as Costa de Carocoles (coast of the seashells), Captiva derives its name from the nefarious doings of the famous pirate Jose Gaspar. The pirate and his band caused a reign of terror in the 1800s by kidnapping people, mostly women, and holding the captives for ransom on the island.

The island also attracted its share of homesteaders in the 1880s. At the tip of the island, where South Seas Plantation is now, Tobe Bryant grew sugar cane, avocados and limes. The produce was kept in a warehouse that has now been magnificently renovated for the King's Crown Dining Room. The old warehouse was ideally located just a few yards from the docks. It was here that they loaded the fruits and vegetables that were shipped to the New York market and other ports.

The entrance to the King's Crown Dining Room is almost obscured by the lush vegetation. Except for the old brick fireplace, the inside gives not a hint that it once functioned as a warehouse. Now, stained-glass windows, crystal chandeliers and mauve-colored print draperies are as inviting as the ocean views.

Their lovely pink linen tablecloths and delicate floral china could enhance any dish. My companion and I began with an appetizer called A Taste of Americana. This is a wonderful trio of red salmon, black sturgeon and golden trout caviar served with condiments. We found that an excellent French Mersault wine was its ideal complement. To cleanse the palate, they served a tangy Key Lime Sorbet.

We then moved on to a Stone Crab Croquette. The crabs, caught locally, are served with a zippy Pommery sauce. Our entrée, Plantation Grouper, also a local catch, is sautéed in butter and Key lime juice, producing a piquant flavor. Their Strawberry and Kiwi Flambée is prepared tableside. This is entertaining to watch, and like food cooked over a campfire, it somehow just seems to taste better.

126

The evening was capped with an after-dinner drink from the liqueur cart. We chose an Eau de Vie. The light and fruity pear taste is as pleasing to the palate as the restaurant, in its lush tropical setting, is pleasing to the rest of the senses.

King's Crown Dining Room is located on South Seas Plantation, at the end of Captiva Road on Captiva Island. Dinner is served from 5:30 p.m. until 9:30 p.m. daily from Christmas to June, and Tuesday through Saturday from June to Christmas. Reservations are suggested. Call (813) 472-5111, extension 3350.

KING'S CROWN DINING ROOM'S
PLANTATION GROUPER

2 sticks butter	**4 teaspoons lime juice**
4 8-ounce grouper fillets	**4 ounces Key Lime Butter**
3 eggs, beaten	**(recipe below)**
1 cup flour	

Melt butter in a sauté pan. Dip grouper fillets in egg wash, then in flour. Sauté fillets on both sides until done. Sprinkle lime juice over each fillet. Remove fish to a plate and garnish each serving with Key Lime Butter. Serves 4.

Key Lime Butter:

4 sticks butter	**½ bunch parsley, minced**
2 ounces Key lime juice	

Soften butter and mix with lime juice and parsley until well blended. Yields 2 cups.

KING'S CROWN DINING ROOM'S KEY LIME SORBET

2 cups sugar	**1½ cups Key lime juice**
4 cups water	**2 cups white wine**

Make a simple syrup by combining sugar and water in a saucepan and bringing it to a boil, stirring constantly. Let syrup cool and mix in lime juice and wine. Pour mixture into a

13-by-9-by-2-inch aluminum or steel tray. Cover the tray tightly with aluminum foil and put it in the freezer. Stir sorbet occasionally until completely frozen. Break up and purée in a food processor before serving, if desired. Serves 25 to 30 in tiny sorbet glasses or 4 to 6 as a dessert.

KING'S CROWN DINING ROOM'S
STONE CRAB CROQUETTES

8 medium stone crab claws
1 tablespoon parsley
½ stalk celery
1 stalk green onion
1 teaspoon Cajun seasoning
1½ tablespoons
  mayonnaise

1 tablespoon ground bread
  crumbs
flour for dredging
2 eggs, beaten
1 cup fine bread crumbs
oil for deep-frying

Extract meat from crab shells, saving both points of the claw. Mince the parsley, celery and onion, and combine them in a bowl with the crabmeat, Cajun seasoning, mayonnaise and a tablespoon of bread crumbs. Cover and chill for 1 hour. Divide mixture into 8 parts and roll each part into a 1½- to 2-inch cylinder. Roll in flour, then in egg wash, and then in bread crumbs. Cover, and refrigerate 1 more hour. Stick a claw point firmly in one end of each croquette. Deep-fry in oil heated to 350 degrees for 8 minutes or until golden brown. Serve with Pommery Sauce. Serves 4.

Pommery Sauce:
3 egg yolks
8 ounces clarified butter
pinch of salt
juice of half a lemon

2 drops Worcestershire
  sauce
3 drops Tabasco sauce
1 tablespoon Pommery
  mustard

Place the yolks in the top of a double boiler over hot, but not boiling water, and whisk until frothy and doubled in size. Slowly drizzle clarified butter into the yolk mixture, whisking vigorously. Remove from heat and gently fold in the remaining ingredients. Serve immediately. Yields 1 cup.

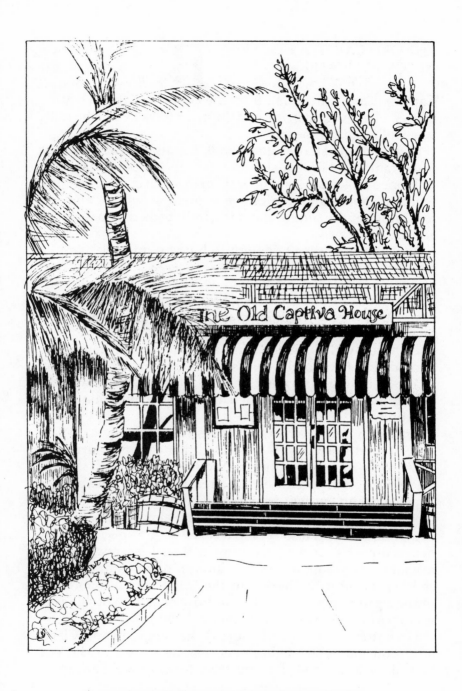

THE OLD CAPTIVA HOUSE
AT 'TWEEN WATERS
Captiva Island

THE OLD CAPTIVA HOUSE
AT 'TWEEN WATERS

Because 'Tween Waters sits at the narrowest point of Captiva Island, stretching from the Gulf Coast to the bay, no matter where you sit in the Old Captiva House, you'll hear the peaceful rolling of the surf.

I watched guest after guest walk through the door of the restaurant and heave a sigh of relief. Its simple, clean, old-fashioned looks just somehow seem to instill confidence. The wooden tables and chairs are a pristine white, and the remainder of the dining room is gently bathed in pale green and salmon tones.

As if the surf wasn't enough to lull you into relaxation, a pianist helps set the mood with semiclassical music. If you become too relaxed, consider the history of the island. I learned that one of the most significant aspects of the island's past is its service as a holding place for prisoners. In the 1500s a seventeen-year-old Spaniard named Juan Ortiz was held prisoner here by the Timacua Indians. He would have been burned alive had not the chief's daughter pleaded for his life. Later she arranged Ortiz's escape to a friendly tribe, and the young man eventually joined de Soto's expedition as an interpreter.

After sampling their Mussels, Oysters Rockefeller and Sausage Stuffed Mushrooms, I decided that each appetizer was good in its own way, but the mushrooms, stuffed with sausage made right on the premises, are a real marvel. In between the appetizers and entrées, I sampled a piece of their homemade bread, which is honestly so good that it almost makes butter superfluous. I was also served a salad with a special creamy house dressing. It was at this point that I learned that the restaurant was built in 1913 as a house in which to tutor the children of John R. Dickey. In the '20s the house and surrounding cottages passed to the Price family, who allowed visitors to vacation here by invitation only!

My entrées arrived and I found the Linguine and Clams most unusual, with a light rather than heavy sauce. The Veal Marsala is also good, but my favorite was their Shrimp de

Jongue. Conversations during this course led to my discovery that Charles and Ann Lindbergh, along with Pulitzer Prize-winning political cartoonist Ding Darling and his wife Penny, were among the "invited." Darling is honored with having the island's wildlife preserve named after him, because he was the first environmentalist in President Franklin Roosevelt's cabinet.

I agonized over which of the seven homemade desserts to choose, but couldn't say no to the moistest Carrot Cake going, or to a taste of their Strawberry Pie with its walnut-macaroon crust. You may favor their old-time Banana Cream Pie, which reminded me of Banana Pudding. And that's the way dining and staying here is—it is one place where, thankfully, nothing is glitzy and new.

The Old Captiva House at 'Tween Waters is located at 15951 Captiva Road on Captiva Island. Breakfast is served from 7:30 a.m. until 11:00 a.m. Monday through Saturday. Lunch is served from 11:00 until midnight Monday through Saturday, from February to April. Dinner is served from 5:30 p.m. until 10:00 p.m. daily. Sunday brunch is served from 9:00 a.m. to 1:00 p.m. during the off-season and from 9:00 a.m. to 2:00 p.m. during season. An Italian buffet is offered Monday night and a Seafood buffet is offered Friday night. For reservations (preferred) call (813) 472-5161.

THE OLD CAPTIVA HOUSE'S SHRIMP DE JONGUE

1½ sticks butter
3 cloves garlic, minced
2 teaspoons flour
28 medium shrimp, peeled
   and deveined

3 tablespoons white wine
1 cup heavy cream
2 teaspoons de jongue
   mustard
¼ cup bread crumbs

Melt butter in a skillet and sauté garlic, flour and shrimp until shrimp turns pink and begins to curl. Remove shrimp and set them aside. Stir in wine, heavy cream and mustard and continue to stir over low heat until sauce begins to thicken. Add cooked shrimp and heat through. Place shrimp on plates and sprinkle with bread crumbs. Serves 4.

THE OLD CAPTIVA HOUSE'S STRAWBERRY PIE

Macaroon Crust:

3 egg whites	**pinch of salt**
1 cup sugar	**1 cup crushed walnuts**
1 teaspoon baking powder	**½ cup cracker meal**

Whip egg whites. As they begin to firm, *slowly* add sugar, baking powder, salt, nuts and cracker meal. The consistency should be that of marshmallow fluff. Spread mixture into a well-greased, 9-inch, deep pie pan and shape it into a crust. Bake at 300 degrees for 30 minutes, or until done.

Filling:
½ pint whipping cream
1 to 1½ pints whole strawberries

Whip cream until stiff. Fold whole strawberries into the cream and pour into cooled pie shell. Try to mound the pie high in the center. Refrigerate for 1 hour before serving. Yields 1 pie.

THE OLD CAPTIVA HOUSE'S LINGUINE AND CLAMS

1 pound linguine pasta	**dash of oregano**
½ cup olive oil	**8 cups chopped, vine-ripe**
2 tablespoons chopped	**tomatoes**
garlic	**24 littleneck clams**
1 tablespoon chopped	**¾ cup white wine**
onions	**2 teaspoons Parmesan**
1 tablespoon chopped	**cheese**
parsley	
basil, salt and pepper to	
taste	

Cook linguine according to package directions; strain and set aside. In a skillet add oil, garlic, onions, parsley, basil, salt, pepper and oregano and cook until onions are clear, about 5 to 6 minutes. Add tomatoes, cover and cook on medium-low heat about 15 minutes. Stir mixture and add clams and wine. Cover until clams pop open. Remove clams from shells and return them to the pan. Discard the shells. Add linguine and sauté for 5 minutes. Top with cheese. Serves 4.

VERANDA
Fort Myers

VERANDA Sitting in the Veranda's tropical courtyard, I sipped a Piña Colada beneath mango trees festooned with hanging wild orchids. As I listened to a gentle waterfall, it was difficult to imagine a time when this oasis, now closed away from the busy city outside, was once the battleground for Seminole Indian uprisings. After the war of 1812, General Andrew Jackson invaded the Spanish colony in retaliation for Indian raiding into Georgia. In 1821, after Spain ceded Florida to the United States for five million dollars, Jackson was made the military governor of Florida. Some twenty years later, during the next Seminole War, a fort was built here and named after Major Myers, who lost his life during an Indian attack.

The Veranda is actually made up of two Victorian Colonial Revival homes, built in 1907 and 1909, that have been joined together by a long kitchen. Reflective of the courtyard, the interior is elegantly decorated in muted green Victorian floral prints. At the side door of one dining room you can see their overproducing herb garden, which supplies all the restaurant's fresh herbs and occasional extras.

Inside, I sat opposite a double-fronted brick fireplace in what had been part of the wraparound veranda. A large mound of fresh-baked bread was soon brought to me with the Veranda's own homemade Pepper Jelly. My next delight was their Crab Bisque. The Veranda has their own deep-sea fishing boat, the *Veranda Ketch*, which supplied the grouper that served as the centerpiece of my Grilled Grouper Salad. This dish was innovative and delicious, making me doubt that catching the fish was as enjoyable as eating it. I then tasted a lemony butterflied Shrimp Salad with crunchy nuts and croutons. Another inventive dish is their Vegetable Napoleon. It's a combination of vegetables stuffed in a pastry puff and smothered in three different cheeses. If you order Boarding House Chicken for lunch you won't want or need dinner because generous portions of chicken, eggplant stuffing and cream sauce go into this yummy dish.

For dessert, and I salivate remembering it, I had their famous Peanut Butter Fudge Pie that tasted similar to, but better than, a Reece's Cup. But you might prefer one of their cobblers; the Blueberry Cobbler is made in the old style, with no artificial ingredients. And the large servings are just one of many things that lend an old-fashioned appeal to this excellent restaurant.

The Veranda is located at 2122 Second Street in Fort Myers. Lunch is served from 11:00 a.m. until 2:30 p.m. Monday through Friday. Dinner is served from 5:30 p.m. until 10:30 p.m. Monday through Thursday, and until 11:30 p.m. on Friday and Saturday. Facilities are available for the handicapped. For reservations (recommended) call (813) 332-2065.

VERANDA'S VEGETABLE NAPOLEON

2 sheets puff pastry
  (commercial)
6 tablespoons butter
6 tablespoons plain flour
2 cups scalded milk
2 tablespoons shredded
  American cheese
2 tablespoons shredded
  Cheddar cheese

2 tablespoons shredded
  Swiss cheese
salt to taste
freshly ground nutmeg to
  taste
1 pound fresh vegetables
  (broccoli, cauliflower,
  snow peas, etc.)

Take 2 sheets of puff pastry and cut them into 2- inch-by-3-inch squares. Roll out on a floured board and bake on a greased baking sheet according to package directions until done, and set aside. Melt butter in a skillet, lower heat, and stir in flour until lumps are dissolved. Gradually pour in scalded milk, stirring to incorporate. Add cheeses, stirring until melted and well mixed. Season this sauce with salt and nutmeg; set aside. Blanch vegetables in boiling water, then remove them from the water. Grease a 1- to 1½-quart shallow baking dish. Place a square of puff pastry on the bottom. Add a layer of blanched vegetables and cover with cheese sauce. Repeat this layering procedure once, then place the dish in a preheated, 350-degree oven for 10 to 15 minutes, until bubbly. Serves 4 to 6.

VERANDA'S BOARDING HOUSE CHICKEN

½ stick butter
2 cups cubed eggplant
¼ cup chopped onions
¾ cup sliced fresh
  mushrooms
2 teaspoons chicken base
pinch of basil

pinch of thyme
pinch of pepper
1 egg, beaten
½ cup bread crumbs
4 tablespoons butter
4 6-ounce deboned chicken
  breasts, skinned

Melt butter in a sauté pan and sauté eggplant, onions and mushrooms together with the chicken base until vegetables are tender. Add spices. Place this mixture in a bowl and let it cool. Add the egg to the mixture and stir in bread crumbs until well mixed. Generously grease a steel platter or heavy baking pan with butter. Place a half cup of stuffing on the platter and cover with a chicken breast. Continue with stuffing and chicken breasts until all are assembled. Bake in a 325-degree oven for about 40 to 45 minutes. Baste chicken breasts with drippings often to prevent drying out. Ladle sauce over top of chicken and serve. Serves 4.

Sauce:
5 tablespoons butter
1 teaspoon chopped
  shallots
1 tablespoon chopped
  onions
pinch of thyme
pinch of rosemary

1 cup heavy cream
½ tablespoon chicken base
2 tablespoons Riesling
  wine (or similar white
  wine)
3 tablespoons flour

Melt 2 tablespoons of the butter in a skillet and sauté shallots, onions and spices until transparent. Stir in heavy cream until incorporated. Add chicken base and stir in white wine; lower heat. In another skillet make a roux by melting the remaining butter and stirring in flour to make a paste. Add a tablespoon of roux at a time to the sauce until sauce reaches desired consistency. Serve hot.

THE PELICAN RESTAURANT AND INN
Fort Myers Beach

THE PELICAN RESTAURANT AND INN

The Pelican came into existence in 1927 when Anna Turner unceremoniously pulled her houseboat up on the beach of Estero Island and proclaimed her houseboat a restaurant and inn. She had added a porch to the boat, where meals of fresh seafood were served to the guests who lived upstairs in the crow's nest. The concept hasn't changed much, although sophisticated sauces have been added to the seafood menu, and guests now stay in cottages along the beach. But this isn't a tale about an unpretentious-looking houseboat; it's a story about its guests, who have faithfully returned here, some for more than twenty-five years. It is they who give this part of the island and the Pelican their character.

In a way they have a kind of club to which I would like to belong. When you stay and dine at the Pelican compound, you become part of the Pelican family and have Pelican friends, who refer to you as a Pelicanite. And, as in all families, there are unwritten rules. An interesting one is the seating arrangement in the nautical dining room, whose wall of windows resemble the ribs of a boat. You only get to sit by the window and watch passing boats silhouetted against the amber sunsets when you have seniority. As the years roll by, repeat guests gradually move closer to graduating to one of the prized window seats.

I graduated quickly, not because of merit but because I came after the lunch hour. I was able to watch the sandpipers scurry across the beach as an occasional sea gull dipped down to search for prey. Even the pelicans made an appearance, and I'm told that one, named Phyllis, will come when called by a favored guest. I gleaned these tidbits while enjoying an exquisite Sherry She-crab Soup. After that wonderful introduction to the Pelican's fare, I was primed for two contrasting seafood concoctions. The first was their Sole Marschel, which is a dainty delicacy made of layers of sole, crabmeat, shrimp and scallops that are baked with Swiss cheese and served with a Béarnaise sauce. The other was baked Grouper Maîson, covered with brown sugar, pineapple and bananas and accented with béarnaise. I have to admit, this dish definitely won over my sweet tooth.

After my tour of the old upstairs dormitory, I gravitated back to my unearned window seat. A slice of Esther's Key Lime Pie was waiting. Esther and Attic Reasoner became the owners of the Pelican in 1959, but their responsibilities have since been passed on to their sons, Buzz and Phil. Both work to maintain a casual ambiance and warm spirit that make repeat guests feel like they are part of a family.

The Pelican Restaurant and Inn is located at 3040 Estero Boulevard in Fort Myers Beach on Estero Island. Two meals are served each day. Lunch is served from 11:30 a.m. until 2:00 p.m., and dinner from 5:00 p.m. until 11:00 p.m. From January through April dinner is served from 4:30 p.m. until 11:00 p.m., with a brunch offered on Sunday. Reservations are not accepted, but the telephone number is (813) 463-6130.

THE PELICAN'S GROUPER MAISON

4 6-ounce grouper fillets	1 cup Béarnaise Sauce
4 bananas	(recipe follows)
5 ounces pineapple juice	6 ounces vegetable oil
4 ounces light brown sugar	4 ounces sliced almonds
4 ounces seasoned bread	4 lemon wedges
crumbs	4 sprigs fresh parsley

Wash fillets in fresh water and let them air dry for 10 minutes. Purée bananas in a blender or by hand, and coat each fillet on both sides with banana purée. Place coated fillets on a greased baking sheet. Pour pineapple juice over and around fillets and top with brown sugar and bread crumbs. Bake in a 350-degree oven for 15 to 18 minutes or until fish begins to flake. Meanwhile, in a skillet heat oil to 350 degrees and sauté the almonds until light brown. Place almonds on paper towels to drain. Arrange fillets on serving plates and pour 2 ounces of Béarnaise Sauce over each. Top each fillet with almonds and garnish with a lemon wedge and parsley. Serves 4.

THE PELICAN'S SOLE MARSCHEL

1½ sticks butter
4 ounces bay scallops
4 ounces shrimp, cut into
 ¼-inch pieces
4 ounces crabmeat (blue,
 stone or Alaskan),
 cooked

16 ounces sole (grey or
 lemon)
8 ounces Swiss cheese,
 shredded
Béarnaise Sauce (recipe
 below)
4 teaspoons minced parsley
 for garnish

In a skillet melt the butter and add scallops and shrimp. Sauté until done. (Shrimp should be turning pink.) Remove from heat and add crabmeat. Let cool. Drain the butter and place seafood on a paper towel. Grease 4 individual au gratin or casserole dishes. Cut the sole into 2-ounce portions, and place a portion of sole on the bottom of each dish. Place 3 ounces of the seafood mix on top of the sole, and top each dish with remaining 2-ounce portions of sole. Sprinkle Swiss cheese on top of each casserole and bake in a preheated, 350-degree oven for 10 to 13 minutes, or until sole is cooked. Top each dish with a dollop of Béarnaise Sauce and garnish with a teaspoon of parsley. Serves 4.

Béarnaise Sauce:
1 cup butter
4 egg yolks
1 tablespoon lemon juice
1 tablespoon tarragon vinegar

¼ teaspoon salt
1 teaspoon chopped parsley
1 teaspoon onion juice
dash of cayenne pepper

Melt butter, but do not scorch. Place egg yolks and ⅓ of the butter in the top of a double boiler. Keep the water in the bottom of the boiler hot, but not boiling. Stirring constantly, add remaining melted butter as the sauce thickens. Remove from heat and add remaining ingredients, stirring until well incorporated. Yields 1 cup.

THE BREAKERS
Palm Beach

THE BREAKERS   I f there is one name that epito-
mizes the grandeur of Florida's
early glory years, it is The Break-
ers. For kings and presidents, millionaires and socialites,
conference delegates and families on summer weekend packages, The Breakers is a part of Florida's heritage.

It all started with Henry Morrison Flagler. When he built
the railroad down the east coast of Florida, he built hotels
along the way to attract the crowds. After fire destroyed the
Palm Beach Inn, he built a more elaborate wooden structure
called The Breakers in 1903.

For years, private railroad cars brought guests like the
Rockefellers, the Astors, Andrew Carnegie, William Randolph Hearst, President Warren Harding and the duchess of
Marlborough to winter at The Breakers. "The season" would
end February 22 with the George Washington Birthday Ball,
after which the guests would board the train in their finery
and depart.

In 1925, The Breakers was destroyed by fire. A much more
magnificent hotel was constructed on the same oceanfront
site in less than twelve months of round-the-clock work by
twelve hundred craftsmen and seventy-five European artists.
The hotel was designed in the Italian Renaissance style by
Leonard Schultze, architect of the Waldorf-Astoria. It's now
listed on the National Register of Historic Places.

When you visit The Breakers today, you approach the
imposing edifice via a long avenue, which cuts through the
green of golf courses and palm trees. Behind the sculptured
fountain, patterned after the one in the Boboli Gardens in
Florence, rise the twin belvedere towers and arches of the
facade, inspired by the famous Villa Medici in Rome.

Inside, you see the artistry of fine European workmanship
captured in tapestries, solid marble floors, frescoes and
vaulted ceilings. The Florentine Room, where dinner is
served, is magnificent, with a beamed, hand-painted ceiling
similar to the one in the Florentine Palace Davanzate. The
adjoining Circle Dining Room, added in 1927, is painted with
scenes of Italian cities and regions and is highlighted with a

spectacular Venetian chandelier hanging from the circular skylight.

As one might expect in such a setting, the dining is formal and elegant. An award-winning wine cellar contains more than four hundred different vintages. Guests not staying at the hotel on the American Plan pay a set price per person for a five-course dinner. Menu selections include appetizers such as Herring Smitane and Breaded Mushrooms with Tomato Sauce; soups; salads; and entrées such as Loin of Pork Toscanna, Shrimp Louie and Tournedoes of Beef Connoisseur. Desserts range from Vodka Sabayon and Sacher Torte to Key Lime Pie and Seasonal Fruit Tarts.

Dinner is followed by dancing to the live orchestra. As you glide around the floor, you don't have to close your eyes and pretend you're in a palace ballroom; you only have to look up to know you're really there.—B.R.M.

The Breakers is located at One South County Road in Palm Beach. During the "high season," mid-December through April, the Florentine Dining Room serves breakfast from 7:00 to 10:00 a.m., and dinner from 6:00 to 9:30 p.m., with two seatings at 6:00 to 6:45 p.m. and 8:30 to 9:15 p.m. From May through early December, breakfast is served from 7:30 to 10:30 a.m., and dinner is served from 6:30 to 9:30 p.m. For reservations (required), call (305) 655-6611.

THE BREAKERS' SHRIMP TEMPURA

½ cup all-purpose flour
½ cup cornstarch
½ teaspoon salt
1 egg
¼ cup water

¼ cup sherry wine
3 cups salad oil for frying
2 pounds large shrimp,
   cleaned and deveined,
   with tails intact

Sift together flour, cornstarch and salt in a bowl. Beat egg with water and wine. Pour egg mixture into the flour mixture and stir until thoroughly combined, being careful not to overbeat as the batter should be a little lumpy.

Heat oil to 360 degrees in a deep saucepan or electric skillet. Holding each shrimp by the tail, dip in the batter and gently drop a few at a time into the hot oil. When shrimp rise to the surface, turn and cook approximately 3 to 4 minutes until golden brown. Drain and serve immediately with your favorite sauces. Serves 6 to 10.

THE BREAKERS' KEY LIME PIE

Pie Crust:

5 tablespoons shortening	**¼ teaspoon salt**
7 tablespoons cake flour	**1 egg**
2 tablespoons sugar	**3 tablespoons milk**

Mix all the ingredients by hand in a mixing bowl. Shape the dough into a ball. Roll dough out using a floured rolling pin and fit it into a 9-inch pie plate. Prick with a fork around bottom and sides. Bake at 375 degrees for 12 to 15 minutes until light brown.

Filling:

3 egg yolks	**1 cup whipped cream**
5 ounces Key lime juice	**fresh lime slices for**
2 cans sweetened con-	**garnish**
densed milk	

Mix egg yolks, lime juice and condensed milk with an electric mixer until smooth and creamy. Pour into prebaked pie shell and bake for 15 minutes at 350 degrees. Allow pie to cool and top with whipped cream. Decorate with slices of fresh lime. Yields 1 pie.

LA VIEILLE MAISON
Boca Raton

LA VIEILLE MAISON When this Mediterranean-style mansion was built in 1928, it was a model home for celebrated architect Addison Mizner's residential development in Boca Raton. Today, it is a showcase of another sort—a showcase for some of the most exquisite dining in the state of Florida.

La Vieille Maîson, "The Old House," is another of owners Leonce Picot's and Al Kocab's famed restaurants, the others being in Fort Lauderdale and Monterey, California. Originally the home of Mizner's chief engineer, it had been turned into apartments when the restaurateurs bought the building in the mid-1970s. With the help of Fort Lauderdale architect David Martin and the decorating skill of Carolyn Picot, they restored it to grandeur and in 1976 opened their now-famous French restaurant.

When you walk through the wrought-iron gates of the two-story house, with its barrel-tile roof and arched windows, you first enter a tropical world of fountains and gardens. Continue, and you step into a virtual designer's show house, with each high-ceilinged room decorated individually with antiques and *objets d'art*. Unmatched tables—oak here, marble-topped there—are set with fine crystal, china and silver. And everywhere there are fresh flowers, mixed bouquets on the tables, sumptuous arrangements on the sideboards and buffets. Oil paintings, figurines, handcrafted chandeliers, imported tile on the fireplace—the eye is greeted with one delight after another in a profusion of harmoniously blended treasures.

When you're seated, the tuxedoed, European-trained waiter is polite, knowledgeable and gracious, gladly guiding even the most indecisive through the joys of ordering from a menu that soars to culinary heights. The wine list alone is awe-inspiring, drawing on a cellar that contains 120,000 bottles and represents an investment of more than a million dollars.

As is common in all full restaurants in France, the dinner is *prix-fixe*. The set price per person includes five courses, with choices ranging from fresh trout flown in from Idaho, venison from Scotland and pheasant from Vermont to red snapper from Florida waters.

My husband Tom and I began our feast with Saucisson Chaud with Sauce Périgueux, a wonderful sausage mixed with pistachios and baked in filo pastry with a truffle sauce, and Escargots aux Petits Légumes, escargots poached in a creamy wine sauce with slivers of turnips, celery and carrots—unforgettably delicious. Our main course, Trois Médaillons, was a grand tour de force of sauces—a lamb noisette with béarnaise, beef tournedo with marchand de vin and venison tournedo with grand veneur.

The appealing cheese and fruit cart was followed by a salad with an excellent house dressing. And then came dessert! The apple sorbet was blissfully cool and refreshing. And the Crêpe Soufflé au Citron, with its raspberry sauce—which chef Yves Labbé demonstrated on Julia Child's television show—was superb.

After such a meal, you can't help but linger, reveling in the romance of the setting, the perfection of the cuisine.—B.R.M.

La Vieille Maîson is located at 770 East Palmetto Park Road in Boca Raton. Dinner seatings are at 6:00 and 6:30 p.m. and 9:00 and 9:30 p.m. every day. The restaurant is closed Memorial Day and Labor Day. For reservations (required) phone (305) 391- 6701.

LA VIEILLE MAISON'S SALADE FLORIDIENNE

2 large, fresh pink
  grapefruit
1 cup sour cream
1 tablespoon brandy

3 tablespoons ketchup
12 ounces blue or stone
  crabmeat

With a sharp knife, peel the grapefruit and separate the sections so that no skin, pith or pips remain. Mix some of the juice with a cup of sour cream. Add brandy and ketchup to the sour cream. Arrange the grapefruit sections on 6 plates. Place some crabmeat on the middle of each serving and spoon the sour cream sauce on top of each. Serves 6.

LA VIEILLE MAISON'S POMPANO AUX PECANS

2 medium-size pompanos
  (or 1-pound fillets)
milk and flour for coating
  the fillets
2 tablespoons butter
salt and pepper to taste

8 pecans, shelled (6
  crushed, 2 halved)
5 ounces Chardonnay
2 tablespoons heavy cream
fresh parsley for garnish

Fillet and skin the pompanos. Dip them in milk, then in flour. In a 10-inch skillet, melt the butter on medium-high heat. When the foam subsides, arrange the fillets in the pan and season them with salt and black or white pepper. Lightly brown one side (about 2 minutes), then flip the fillets over. Season again and strew the crushed pecans over and around the fish. After about 2 more minutes, add Chardonnay and sprinkle the cream over and around the fish. Reduce the heat to low (the fish must not boil), cover the pan and let the fillets relax in the cooking liquids for a couple more minutes. To serve, place the fillets on heated plates. Slightly reduce the juices left in the skillet and pour over the pompanos. Decorate with the pecan halves and fresh parsley. Serves 2.

CAP'S PLACE
Lighthouse Point

CAP'S PLACE

When the crusty old seafaring owner of Cap's Place was told that his remote, rustic restaurant was needed for a secret dinner party for President Franklin Roosevelt and Prime Minister Winston Churchill, he obliged. But Cap viewed the whole affair as a nuisance, what with all those secret service agents around, recalls Talle Hasis. Talle is the daughter of Cap's partner Al Hasis, and she has run the restaurant for fifteen years.

Churchill had flown to Washington in the winter of 1942 to plan wartime strategies with FDR. When he came down with the flu, he sought the warmth of south Florida to improve his health. He stayed with Under Secretary of State Edward Stettinius, who owned a home across the Intracoastal Waterway from Cap's tiny island. When Roosevelt and General George Marshall arrived, they all went to Cap's Place to eat.

Cap's hasn't changed much since then. In fact, it's much the same as it was in the late 1920s, when a Spanish-American War veteran and fisherman named Captain Eugene Theodore Knight started it all. Cap bought a dredging barge for one hundred dollars in Miami and towed it to a desolate island surrounded by mangrove swamp in what is now Lighthouse Point. He pulled it up on land and built a shack on top as a haven for fishermen. In the next few years he added a house for himself and opened a restaurant, accessible only by boat.

During the thirties, Cap's became a rum-running restaurant and gambling casino. Cap opened the back betting room only for those diners he knew were well-heeled. Water glasses are stored today in the spaces which once held slot machines ready to be dropped into a trapdoor if "the Feds" came.

The restaurant's rugged buildings, made of Dade County pine with exposed beams and rafters, have weathered well. Much to the dismay of some old-time customers, the restaurant is now air-conditioned in the summer, though the windows open wide in cooler weather.

Historical photos and memorabilia line the walls. Of special interest is the mounted skin of a six-foot-long rattlesnake, shot on the island by Al Hasis just as it was about to strike Cap.

150

Chef Donald Brown demonstrated for us how they peel the paper-thin edible portions of the sabal palm, or "swamp cabbage"—bought from a Seminole family in Okeechobee—to make their fresh Hearts of Palm Salad. After tasting this specialty, with its wonderful secret dressing, I could understand why it's so famous.

Oysters, clams, crabs, lobster, shrimp, scallops and the catch of the day—served broiled, deep-fried, pan-fried, sautéed or poached in white wine—have been prepared by the chef, Sylvester Love, for almost fifty years. Though great pasta specials, fried chicken and Island Steak are offered, fresh Florida seafood is what Cap's is all about. That, and the adventure of a boat ride into the past.—B.R.M.

Cap's Place is located on an island a quarter of a mile north of the Hillsboro Inlet, south of Boca Raton. You can catch Cap's launch at the boat dock at 2765 Northeast 28th Court in Lighthouse Point. Dinner is served from 5:30 p.m. to 10:00 p.m. Sunday through Thursday, and from 5:30 p.m. to 11:00 p.m. Friday and Saturday. No reservations are accepted, but the number for information is (305) 941-0418.

CAP'S PLACE'S BLUEFISH DIJON

1 small bluefish fillet (or snapper, grouper or trout)
juice of 1 or 2 lemons

2 tablespoons Dijon Sauce (recipe below)
1 tablespoon margarine

Marinate the fish fillet in lemon juice for 10 minutes. Prepare Dijon Sauce. Dip fish, skin up, into sauce, then place on a heavy, flat, iron skillet that has been greased with a pat of margarine. Let fish cook on medium heat until meat is no longer translucent and turns whitish (5 to 10 minutes or so). Flip fish over and spread Dijon Sauce on top of fish. Warm a few minutes and serve. Serves 1.

Dijon Sauce:
½ cup Dijon mustard
1 cup liquid margarine
1 teaspoon minced fresh garlic

1 tablespoon fresh lemon juice
1 tablespoon paprika

151

Whisk ingredients together until orange-colored. Use for fish or broiled chicken. Store leftover sauce in a covered container in the refrigerator. Serves 8.

CAP'S PLACE'S SEAFOOD LINGUINE

Pasta:

1 pound linguine
3 cups water

3 tablespoons olive oil
½ tablespoon fresh garlic

Cook linguine in boiling water to which olive oil and fresh garlic have been added. Cook al denté; remove from heat. Do not rinse or drain. (Add ice to top to stop further cooking if not using immediately.) Place pasta in casserole dishes, using a pasta scooper so some of the liquid drains out. Top with seafood sauce and Parmesan cheese.

Sauce:

5 tablespoons margarine
1½ tablespoons fresh garlic, finely minced
2 tablespoons fresh parsley, chopped
2½ cups milk
5 tablespoons all-purpose flour
2 pounds of firm, white fish (like grouper or dolphin)

16 medium to large shrimp
1½ pounds fresh scallops
1½ tablespoons sherry
2 tablespoons fresh lemon juice
½ teaspoon paprika
salt to taste
Parmesan cheese to taste

In a saucepan, melt margarine and add minced garlic and parsley. Set aside. Warm the milk and add flour gradually, using a wire whisk to avoid lumps. Whisk until smooth and add to margarine mixture. Put saucepan on medium heat, but do not boil. Cook 5 minutes. Chop fish into bite-size morsels; peel and devein shrimp. Add raw seafood and cook 5 more minutes. Remove from heat. Add sherry and lemon juice. Blend in paprika for color and salt to taste, if desired. Ladle mixture on top of cooked linguine, served in warm, individual casserole dishes. Sprinkle Parmesan cheese on top. Serves 6 to 8.

HISTORIC BRYAN HOMES
RESTAURANT
Fort Lauderdale

HISTORIC BRYAN
HOMES RESTAURANT

Walking up to the Historic Bryan Homes Restaurant in Fort Lauderdale, you can see that is a special place even before you enter. The gracious tree-shaded yard along the New River and the two turn-of-the-century houses create an urban oasis of relaxed Old Florida.

Fort Lauderdale founding father Philomen Bryan built these houses for his sons Thomas and Reed in 1904. Made of poured concrete blocks, with pine floors and brick fireplaces, the homes had a separate kitchen built apart from the main houses.

The Bryan brothers owned the first electric, telephone and water companies in Fort Lauderdale, and Reed Bryan was the second mayor of the city. In 1905 they built near their homes a hotel similar in style to their own residences. This is now the Discovery Center, a hands-on science and history museum.

Declared historic landmarks and restored by the city of Fort Lauderdale in 1981, the houses were leased to entrepreneur and executive chef Anthony Gillette in 1982. He hired architect Randolph Henning to transform them into restaurants, while preserving the character of the buildings. For their efforts, they received an AIA Design Award in 1983 and a Community Appearance Award from the city.

Today, diners can appreciate the charmingly done rooms— decorated with antiques, lace curtains and period wallpaper— as they look out at the river, beautiful at night with shining lights.

The restaurant has specialized in "New Florida cuisine," using only fresh, indigenous items and adding a Caribbean touch. Appetizers include Seafood Pie, Conch and Scallops Seviche, Alligator Bites and Conch Fritters, delicious with a Key lime mustard sauce.

Broiled Swordfish Captiva, Stuffed Veal Cedar Key with andouille sausage and blue cheese, Blackened Pepper Steak and Roast Duckling Duval with raspberry sauce are a few of the many entrées. I especially enjoyed a Fillet of Grouper with peach and mango sauce.—B.R.M.

Historic Bryan Homes Restaurant is located at 301 Southwest Third Avenue in Fort Lauderdale. Dinner hours are from 5:30 to 10:00 p.m. Sunday through Thursday and from 5:30 to 11:00 p.m. on Friday and Saturday. The restaurant is closed Monday. Reservations are suggested; call (305) 523-0177.

HISTORIC BRYAN HOMES RESTAURANT'S BLOODY MARY WHOLE SNAPPER

2 cups chili sauce
½ onion, minced fine
3 cloves fresh garlic, minced
¼ cup Worcestershire sauce
1 teaspoon salt

1 tablespoon Tabasco sauce
¼ cup fresh lime juice
¼ cup vodka
1 teaspoon celery salt
2 bay leaves
1 1½-pound whole snapper

Mix all the ingredients except the snapper. Marinate snapper in this mixture for 2 to 4 hours in the refrigerator. Place snapper in a baking dish and pour marinade over it. Bake at 375 degrees for 15 to 20 minutes. (If desired, serve with yucca chips and fried plantain.) Serves 2.

HISTORIC BRYAN HOMES RESTAURANT'S CONCH FRITTERS

½ pound fresh conch meat, peeled and cleaned
2 cups self-rising flour
¼ Spanish onion, minced fine
½ green pepper, chopped fine
½ red pepper, chopped fine
1 Anaheim chili, minced

1 Cubano bell pepper
¼ cup minced cilantro
1 teaspoon salt
½ teaspoon cayenne pepper
1 teaspoon black pepper
1 tablespoon ground cumin seeds
¼ cup clam juice
¼ cup oil

Grind conch meat until fine in a processor. Add remaining ingredients, except oil, and blend well. Form mixture into half-dollar-size patties and sauté in oil until golden brown, about 5 to 7 minutes, turning as sides brown. Serves 4 to 6.

155

HISTORIC BRYAN HOMES RESTAURANT'S MILE-HIGH KEY LIME TARTLETTE

3 egg yolks
1 can sweetened condensed
  milk

juice of 6 limes
grated outer rind of 6 limes
1 9-inch pie shell, baked

Beat egg yolks in a bowl until they are thick and form a ribbon when dripped from the spoon. Add condensed milk and continue to beat on low speed. Then mix in the lime juice and grated rind. Chill overnight.

Fill a baked pastry pie shell with the lime mixture. Top with Italian Meringue and place under a broiler for 2 minutes, turning as meringue browns. Serve on top of Strawberry Purée. Serves 8.

Italian Meringue:

1 cup sugar
¼ cup water

6 egg whites
pinch of cream of tartar

Cook sugar and water until mixture reaches 248 degrees on a candy thermometer or until mixture forms a soft ball when dripped from a spoon into water. Beat egg whites with a pinch of cream of tartar until they are stiff. Add the sugar mixture, taking care not to pour it on the beaters. Beat on high speed until egg whites are stiff and shiny. Put the meringue in a pastry bag and pipe it (very high) on the pie, or dollop it with a spoon.

Strawberry Purée:

1 pint strawberries   ¼ cup sugar

Purée strawberries with the sugar in a blender until liquified. Put a few spoonfuls on a plate and top with a slice of Key Lime Tartlette.

CASA VECCHIA
Fort Lauderdale

CASA VECCHIA

When Leonce Picot and art designer Al Kocab started to write a book entitled "100 Great Restaurants of the U.S.," they couldn't find a hundred that met their standards. So they decided to open one of their own.

They now run three entirely different, and universally praised, restaurants—La Vieille Maîson in Boca Raton, and the Down Under and Casa Vecchia in Fort Lauderdale.

Casa Vecchia, which means "old house" in Italian, is in the last house remaining on Birch Avenue, and it probably would have become another condo if the partners hadn't purchased it. Built between 1936 and 1938 by heirs of the Ponds Cold Cream fortune, the house was later owned by Stephen J. O'Connell, a Florida Supreme Court justice and a chancellor of the University of Florida. The house also served as an office building for a private hospital at one time.

When Leonce Picot and Al Kocab began their renovation, the house was eaten up with termites; sixty percent of the interior and back walls had to be replaced. Striving to create a feeling "of a comfortable home on the Riviera," they filled the many rooms and nooks and crannies and porches with a feast of visual delights. Antique wood paneling designed by Tiffany, Venetian-glass lights, oil paintings and lithographs, the original fireplace, antiques from Europe, fresh flowers and a view of the Intracoastal Waterway only a few feet away create a sumptuous setting.

Casa Vecchia is considered by many food critics to be among the finest Italian restaurants in the country. Each dish is a joy to look at—and to eat. The pasta is all made on the premises, and all ingredients are absolutely fresh, some being specially flown in. Hundreds of fine wines are offered.

The only problem is choosing from the extensive menu and the daily specials. Carpaccio or Shrimp Marsala? Cold Cream of Broccoli or Fresh Mussel Soup? Capellini d'Angelo (angel hair noodles with a tomato cream sauce, peas and prosciutto) or perhaps a dish of Caviar and Linguine? And there are seafood entrées to tempt you, like Snapper Bourguignonne, Fresh Trout with Pine Nuts or Crabmeat Casa Vecchia. Not to mention the veal, lamb, beef and chicken dishes, such as Petto di Pollo Ripièno alla Genovese, a breast of chicken stuffed with chopped veal, spinach, pistachios and spices.

Difficult though such decision making may be, you can be assured that there are no wrong answers. My Mushroom Fettucine was delicious, as was the Shrimp Riviera, sautéed to perfection. For dessert, their Hazelnut Praline Mousse was heaven, and their Amaretto Cake celestial as well.—B.R.M.

Casa Vecchia is located at 209 North Birch Road in Fort Lauderdale. Dinner is the only meal served. Hours are from 6:00 to 10:00 p.m. Sunday through Thursday, and until 10:30 p.m. on Friday and Saturday. For reservations (suggested) call (305) 463-7575.

CASA VECCHIA'S ALLA NOCCIOLA
(Hazelnut Praline Mousse)

1 pound sugar	**4 ounces Frangelica liqueur**
½ pound hazelnuts	**4 egg whites**
1 pint heavy cream	

To make the praline, cook ½ pound of the sugar in a heavy skillet. Stir it until light brown. Add hazelnuts and cook for 2 more minutes. Pour mixture in a lightly oiled sheet pan. Let the mixture cool. When praline is hard, break it in small pieces and grind it (not too fine) in a food processor.

To make the mousse, whip heavy cream; add liqueur and remaining sugar. In a separate bowl, next whip egg whites until stiff. Fold all ingredients together very lightly, reserving ½ cup of praline for a garnish. Spoon mousse into serving glasses. Sprinkle leftover praline on top. Chill in refrigerator for 2 hours before serving. Serves 8.

CASA VECCHIA'S SHRIMP RIVIERA

2 pounds large prawns	**¼ teaspoon salt**
1 ounce olive oil	**¼ teaspoon freshly ground**
2 tablespoons butter	**pepper**
1 small garlic clove,	**juice of 2 lemons**
crushed	**2 ounces dry vermouth**

Shell the prawns, leaving the tails on. Put the olive oil in a large skillet and heat. When simmering, add shrimp and cook until golden brown. Reduce heat and add butter, garlic, salt and pepper. (When you think you have too much salt, add more. This is one dish you can hardly oversalt.) When well blended, raise heat to very hot. Add lemon juice and dry vermouth. Cook about 1 minute, constantly stirring or shaking. Serves 4 as an appetizer or 2 as an entrée.

CASA VECCHIA'S TROTA ALA PRIMAVERA
(Trout Primavera)

2 medium carrots
1 zucchini
handful of snow peas
1 green pepper
1 small onion
2 stalks celery
1 stick sweet butter
2 tablespoons fresh basil
   (optional)

salt and pepper to taste
2 12- to 14-ounce trout,
   boned and filleted (fresh
   if possible)
¼ cup milk
flour for dusting
3 cups classic hollandaise
   sauce
½ cup whipping cream

Clean and cut vegetables (substitutions are fine) in small julienne strips. In a large skillet, melt butter on high heat and add vegetables, in order, for necessary cooking time. (For example, first add carrots, then celery, green peppers, etc.) No water or juice is needed. Season with basil, salt and pepper. Cook for 8 to 10 minutes. Vegetables should be firm and crunchy.

Dip trout in milk and dust with flour. Sauté on both sides until nice and brown. Place trout on a flat pan; top with vegetables. Set aside. (Steps up to this point may be made one day ahead. Refrigerate of course.) Mix hollandaise with whipping cream for a mousseline sauce. Just before serving, heat trout in a moderate oven for 3 to 5 minutes. (If trout has been refrigerated, heat longer.) Remove, place on plates and spoon mousseline sauce over top. Serves 4.

JOE'S STONE CRAB
Miami Beach

JOE'S STONE CRAB

Almost as long as there has been a Miami Beach, there has been a Joe's. Joseph Weiss, an asthmatic waiter in New York, moved to Miami in 1913 for his health. His short-order counter at Smith's Casino, a popular bathing spot, grew into a restaurant in 1918 when he started serving "shore dinners" on the wooden front porch of his family bungalow on the south end of Miami Beach.

In 1921, as Miami Beach entered the era of boom development, a visiting scientist asked Joe to cook a stone crab, a crustacean found in abundance but scorned by natives because of its odd taste and slimy texture. Joe cooked it, and then he chilled it, and that made all the difference. What had been an unpleasant-tasting meat when hot became, when cold, a sweet and succulent delicacy.

Joe started serving his cold stone crabs with melted butter and a mustard sauce, and presidents, royalty, celebrities, millionaires and just hungry folks have been queuing up ever since—and with "no reservations accepted," lines are a tradition.

Along with culinary success has come media attention. Beginning in the 1930s with Damon Runyon, writers, critics and gossip columnists have all covered Joe's, and television and movie directors have even used it in their scripts.

Joe's Stone Crab today is a big enterprise, with its own fishing fleet providing the restaurant with a ton of stone crab claws a day and shipping more across the country and to Japan. Only the claws are harvested; the live crab is returned to the water to regenerate new claws.

There is only one Joe's Stone Crab restaurant; there are no franchises, no branches, no clones. Located in a large stucco building with Mediterranean touches, the restaurant can seat up to four hundred at a time. The main dining room, built in 1930, is simply decorated, with terrazzo and black-and-white tile floors and enormous photos of the Weiss family on the wall. Mahogany woodwork, a wrought-iron chandelier and a painted ceiling adorn the newer Garden Room.

Joann Weiss Sawitz, Joe's granddaughter, is an elegant executive who oversees one hundred and seventy employees with warmth and firmness. A cook herself from the age of twelve, she has a special test kitchen beside her office where she teaches the staff new dishes. She told me that it was her recipe, created when she was seventeen years old, that her father Jesse chose when he quickly had to find a Key Lime Pie after a Chicago restaurant critic raved about the one served at Joe's—when they offered none. It is now internationally acclaimed, and a closely guarded secret.

Though stone crabs are trademarks of Joe's, there is an abundant selection of other seafood as well, from fresh broiled snapper and pompano to shrimp, oysters, frog legs and lobster. There are also salads and great vegetables, and even a smattering of meat entrées for the truly foolish.—B.R.M.

Joe's Stone Crab is located at 227 Biscayne Street in Miami Beach. Lunch is served from 11:30 a.m. to 2:00 p.m. Tuesday through Saturday. Dinner is served daily from 5:00 p.m. to 10:00 p.m. The restaurant is closed from mid-May to mid-October. No reservations are accepted, but for information call (305) 673- 0365.

JOE'S STONE CRAB'S VINAIGRETTE SALAD DRESSING

¼ cup chopped onions (or scallions)
3 tablespoons minced parsley
2 tablespoons chopped pimiento
1 hard-boiled egg, chopped
2 tablespoons minced chives

1½ teaspoons sugar
1 teaspoon salt
½ teaspoon red pepper
⅓ cup vinegar
¾ cup of olive oil
½ cup capers (optional)

Mix all the ingredients together. Serve on salads. Refrigerate leftover dressing. Yields approximately 2 cups.

JOE'S STONE CRAB'S COTTAGE FRIED SWEET POTATOES

4 sweet potatoes
1 quart vegetable oil

salt to taste

163

Peel and cut the potatoes into slices that are as thin as potato chips, using a mandoline or the slicing blade of a food processor. Soak slices in ice water until you're ready to prepare and serve them. Heat the oil in a fryer or electric frying pan to 400 degrees. Blot the sweet potato slices dry and fry them for 2 minutes, or until crisp and golden brown. Remove with a slotted spoon and drain on paper towels. Sprinkle with salt and serve at once. Serves 4 to 6.

JOE'S STONE CRAB'S MUSTARD SAUCE

3½ teaspoons Colman's dry
   English mustard
1 cup mayonnaise
2 teaspoons Worcestershire
   sauce

1 teaspoon A-1 sauce
2 tablespoons light cream
⅛ teaspoon salt

Combine the mustard and mayonnaise in a bowl and beat for 1 minute. Add the remaining ingredients and beat until smooth and creamy. Serve as an accompaniment to fresh stone crab claws which have been cracked with a wide-headed mallet. Yields 1¼ cups.

JOE'S STONE CRAB'S GRILLED TOMATOES

4 beefsteak tomatoes
2 cups creamed spinach
   (your favorite recipe)
3 cups seasoned bread
   crumbs

¾ cup melted butter
salt and pepper to taste
1½ cups grated mild
   Cheddar cheese

Cut each tomato into 3 thick slices and arrange on an oiled baking sheet. Combine creamed spinach with bread crumbs, butter, salt and pepper. (The mixture should be thick.) Spread each tomato slice with the spinach mixture and sprinkle with grated cheese. Place the tomatoes under a broiler and cook until the cheese is melted and golden brown. Serves 4 to 6.

TOBACCO ROAD
Miami

TOBACCO ROAD

Liquor license 0001—the first in Dade County—is held by Tobacco Road. Built as a bar in Miami in 1912, this drinking establishment has led a wild and crazy life. A speakeasy during Prohibition, it was the reported hangout of Al Capone. It was also an illegal gambling casino, raided by ax-wielding policemen. During World War II it was put off limits to military personnel for encouraging "lewd and lascivious conduct." It was, as a sign in the present-day Tobacco Road says, "a constant source of anguish to law enforcement agencies."

Five years ago, when Patrick Gleber and Kevin Rusk were running a restaurant in an expensive suburban shopping center, they were approached by friend and realtor Michael Lattener to do a feasibility study on purchasing a "beat-up little dive." Though the immediate neighborhood had seen better days, the building was within a few blocks of booming Brickell Avenue with all its gleaming new skyscrapers and international banks.

"Everyone thought we were crazy," Kevin Rusk recalls, but the three went together and purchased Tobacco Road. They redid much of the interior, though the front is still long and narrow and dark, and they made the rear patio into an appealing biergarten-type dining area.

Since then, they have been packing in evening crowds for their Chicago blues entertainment, and they have been drawing crowds of professionals at lunch for the great food.

Tobacco Road is well known for its burgers—they freshly grind their own beef and make patties by hand—and for their cut-to-order french fries. But the chef, John Kregg, a graduate of the Culinary Institute of America, goes far beyond that, offering homemade soups, salads, pasta and seafood specials, as well as delicious desserts.

On the day I was there with friends, sitting on the terrace under an enormous old oak, I ordered a wonderfully prepared Mushroom Soup. The day's special, Escargot Provençale served with linguine, was superb. So was the Curried Chicken Salad, judged the best in South Florida by a local magazine.

166

The owners are especially proud of their homemade ice cream, offering interesting flavors such as carambola and cinnamon chocolate. Though they had sold out of ice cream when I was there, we all overcame our disappointment quickly when we tasted the Key Lime Pie and delicious Chocolate Tart.—B.R.M.

Tobacco Road is located at 626 South Miami Avenue in Miami. Hours are from 11:30 a.m. to 5:00 a.m. No reservations are necessary. For information call (305) 374-1198.

TOBACCO ROAD'S ESCARGOT PROVENCALE

1 tablespoon olive oil
6 to 8 escargots
1 teaspoon garlic, finely
   chopped
¼ green pepper, diced
½ tomato, peeled, seeded
   and diced

1 teaspoon fresh basil,
   chopped
salt and pepper to taste
¼ cup white wine
6 ounces fresh linguine,
   cooked

Heat olive oil in a sauté pan. Add escargots and garlic and sauté lightly. Add peppers, tomatoes and basil and sauté until tender but crisp. Add salt, pepper and wine. Bring to a boil, then pour over cooked pasta. Serves 1.

TOBACCO ROAD'S CARAMBOLA ICE CREAM

3 to 4 ripe carambola
   (starfruit)
2½ cups milk
2 cups heavy cream

1½ cups sugar
3 egg yolks
4 teaspoons vanilla

Cut the fruit into slices. Purée carambola in a food processor with half of the milk. In a mixing bowl, combine all the ingredients and mix with a whisk until the sugar dissolves. Pour the mixture into an ice-cream machine and let it run until the mixture is smooth, creamy and thick (without a granular texture). Take the ice cream out of the machine and let it harden in the freezer; or it can be eaten as is. Yields ½ gallon.

TOBACCO ROAD'S SAUTEED CONCH STEAKS WITH LIME BUTTER AND SAUTEED ALMONDS

6 to 8 ounces conch steak
salt and pepper to taste
¼ cup flour
2 tablespoons butter

1¼ cup white wine
1 tablespoon lime juice
1 tablespoon smoked
  almonds

Pound conch steaks to tenderize. Season with salt and pepper and dust with flour. Melt 1 tablespoon of butter in a sauté pan and sauté conch about 3 minutes per side, or until done. Remove steaks from pan and keep warm; add wine, lime juice and almonds to the pan. Cook until the liquid reduces. Add the remaining tablespoon of butter and shake the pan until butter melts to make a sauce. Check seasoning and adjust if necessary. Pour over conch steaks and serve. Serves 1.

CHARADE
Coral Gables

CHARADE

Much of the ornately carved furniture that was found in early Coral Gables homes, churches and hotels came not from Old World Spain but from the Granada Shops on Ponce de Leon Circle, the site of today's Charade restaurant.

When George Merrick planned his Mediterranean development of Coral Gables in the 1920s, he included a craft section to house and to provide workshops for the craftsmen who would furnish the buildings of his community. Designed by Phineas Paist, these buildings were intended to be quaint counterparts of those in Italy and Spain.

The Granada Shops was a furniture shop in the craft section. It was one of the success stories of Merrick's plan. Constructed in 1925, the building was owned by brothers Ralph and Leland Wilkins, who employed carvers from Spain, Italy, France, Germany and Cuba. The family of Ralph Wilkins lived on the second floor, with a workshop and large showroom downstairs. The barrel-tile roof was damaged in the killer hurricane of 1926, which wiped out much of Miami, but the stucco building has survived intact ever since.

In 1939 the University of Miami purchased the building and used it for a Navy Officers Training School, then for band classes and rehearsals of the Music Department. It was a fraternity house and coffeehouse before being sold in the late 1950s to Lou Paoletti for an Italian restaurant.

The current owner, Hagen Taudt, who also owns the Kaleidoscope restaurant in Coconut Grove, bought the building in 1976. After doing renovation work, he inaugurated Charade in May 1977.

With its awnings and flowers on the windowsills and balcony, Charade is charming on the outside, and even more so on the inside. When you enter the main dining area, you are immediately struck with the mellowness of the old terracotta tile floors and the rich, dark beams of the two-story cypress ceiling. Oil paintings, chintz-covered chairs, a grand piano, hand-carved mahogany doors and a cascade of potted palms in the center of the room create an atmosphere George Merrick surely would have appreciated.

170

German-born, Hagen Taudt is a trained chef who has worked in Europe, Africa and Canada, as well as in the United States. His menu reflects his cosmopolitan background. Selections include Senegalese Soup, Linguine con Frutti di Mare, Medaillons of Veal aux Trois Champignons and Noisettes of Venison "Grand Veneur," this last served with wild mushrooms, pineapple and red currants in a red wine sour cream sauce. In addition, the restaurant offers local seafood specialties, such as a fresh fish of the day served à la meunière, Grilled Swordfish au Buerre de Crevettes and Fillet of Red Snapper "Vert-Pre."

For lunch I selected from their many salads the Avocado Ritz, avocado halves filled with a mixture of shrimp, crab and scallops. And I couldn't forgo another dessert from those ever-tempting pastry carts, this time a Napoleon made by Charade's pastry chef.—B.R.M.

Charade is located at 2900 Ponce de Leon Boulevard in Coral Gables. Lunch is served Monday through Friday from 11:30 a.m. to 3:00 p.m. Dinner is served from 6:30 p.m. to 11:00 p.m. Monday through Thursday, from 6:00 p.m. to midnight Friday and Saturday, and from 6:00 p.m. to 10:30 p.m. Sunday. A Sunday buffet brunch is served from 11:30 a.m. to 3:00 p.m. For reservations (suggested) call (305) 448-6077.

CHARADE'S BRAISED RABBIT AU CALVADOS

2 4- to 5-pound rabbits, skinned and cleaned
1 teaspoon rosemary
salt and pepper to taste
¼ cup flour
½ cup butter
½ cup diced onions
1 garlic clove, crushed
¾ cup diced carrots
2 tablespoons tomato paste
¼ cup flour
¼ cup Calvados (apple brandy)
1 cup dry white wine
1½ cups chicken stock (or bouillon)
1 tablespoon chopped chives

Cut up each rabbit by first removing the front and hind legs. Then remove the neck and rib cage and discard. Cut up the

171

back or saddle of each rabbit into 4 pieces; wash under cold water and pat dry. Rub each piece with rosemary, salt and pepper and dip in flour. Melt butter in large, heavy, iron braising skillet and pan-fry meat to a golden brown. Add the diced onions and crushed garlic and sauté 2 to 3 minutes. Add the carrots and tomato paste, then dust the meat and vegetables with ¼ cup flour. After turning several times and browning lightly, pour in Calvados and flambée to burn off most of the alcohol. Then add white wine and a little later the chicken stock. Braise the meat over low to medium heat for approximately an hour, or until tender. To serve, garnish with chopped chives. Serves 4.

CHARADE'S SAUTEED SHRIMP AND SCALLOPS SUR LIT D'EPINARD

2½ pounds of fresh spinach
1 teaspoon chopped garlic
1 cup of butter, divided into
 thirds
salt and pepper to taste
12 extralarge shrimp,
 peeled and deveined

24 scallops, patted dry
3 tablespoons curry
 powder
¼ cup brandy
½ cup white wine
2 or 3 drops Tabasco sauce

Wash spinach several times and pat dry. Sauté spinach leaves and garlic in ⅓ cup butter for just a few minutes. Leaves still must be slightly crisp. Add salt and pepper to taste. Remove from heat and keep warm. Simultaneously sauté the shrimp and scallops in ⅓ cup of the butter for approximately 2 to 3 minutes. Dust with curry powder and flambée with brandy. Add the white wine, a dash of salt and pepper and a few drops of Tabasco. Let the seafood simmer for 2 to 3 minutes. Divide spinach onto 4 plates and spread it out. Remove shrimp and scallops from the skillet and arrange on spinach leaves. Quickly bring the sauce to a boil and whip into the sauce the last ⅓ cup of soft butter. Pour sauce over shrimp and scallops and serve immediately. Serves 4.

RESTAURANT ST. MICHEL
Coral Gables

RESTAURANT ST. MICHEL

When Stuart Bornstein graduated from law school, he didn't set out his shingle; he founded his own crêperie. In partnership with Alan Potamkin, he opened the Crêpe St. Michel in Coral Gables in 1974. Since then, he has expanded his dining establishment into a full restaurant, a bar and lounge, and an exquisite small hotel with individually furnished rooms. Polishing and perfecting along the way, he has created a nostalgic corner of European charm at his Hotel Place St. Michel.

Designed by Anthony Zinc, the Mediterranean-style, three-story building features a dramatic entrance, balconies and a roof-top tower. It was constructed in 1926 for offices and stores, at a cost of $25,000. Soon afterwards, it became the Hotel Seville. During the 1960s it was "modernized," with dropped ceilings, fluorescent lighting and Danish modern furniture.

Stuart Bornstein has painstakingly restored the building to show off the original Spanish tile, the parquet floors, the arched ceilings and windows. The French doors, the mahogany bar, the Art Nouveau lights from an old theater in Miami, the antiques and the artwork all blend together in an Old World melange.

The Restaurant St. Michel, just off the lobby of the hotel, is a casually elegant and popular dining spot, unintimidating enough for teen-agers on special dates, yet sophisticated enough for international visitors to find enticing.

The hardwood floors and wooden chairs and tables are reminiscent of French bistros. A brass teller's cage from an old bank accents the espresso coffee station. A white baby grand occupies a place of prominence, ready for the pianist who plays nightly and the jazz duo who play for Sunday brunch.

Though manager Greg O'Leary emphasizes that their menu goes far beyond just crêpes these days, covering a variety of French and continental dishes, I still love what made them famous. Their Crêpe à l'Indienne, made with curried chicken topped with coconut, almonds and chutney, is a personal favorite.

Appetizers range from Huîtres (oysters) Bienville and Steak Tartare to Escargots de Bourgogne. Seafood entrées include Snapper au Basil, fresh Florida lobster in a spinach cream sauce (Homard au gratin St. Michel) and poached salmon (Saumon Poché au Champagne et Oseille). Among other entrées are Steak Poivre Crème, Canard au Cassis and a delicious veal with wine, mushrooms, cream and mustard called Escalopine de Veau Dijonnaise.

For dessert, you may order a chocolate mousse, a fresh pastry, a flambée or a crêpes sucrées. I'll take the Crêpe Chocolat Chantilly à la Mode, s'il vous plaît.—B.R.M.

Restaurant St. Michel is located in the Hotel Place St. Michel at 162 Alcazar Avenue in Coral Gables. Breakfast is served from 7:00 a.m. to 9:30 a.m. Monday through Friday; lunch and dinner are served from 11:00 a.m. to 11:00 p.m. Monday through Thursday; from 11:00 a.m. to 1:00 a.m. Friday and Saturday; and from 6:00 p.m. to 11:00 p.m. on Sunday. Sunday brunch is served from 11:00 a.m. to 2:30 p.m. Reservations are recommended; call (305) 446-6572.

RESTAURANT ST. MICHEL'S SALMON WITH GINGER CREAM SAUCE

4 6-ounce salmon steaks	½ stick butter
1 cup white wine	juice of 2 oranges
3 laurel leaves	6 ounces lowfat plain yogurt
dash of thyme	
2 shallots	3 ounces cream cheese
1 ounce fresh ginger	salt and pepper to taste

Place salmon in poaching pan and cover with white wine and enough cold water to cover fish. Add laurel leaves and thyme. Bring to a boil and immediately turn off the heat. Allow salmon to sit in the pan for 5 minutes. Meanwhile, sauté shallots and ginger in butter for 2 minutes, until golden. Add orange juice, yogurt and cream cheese. Stir and cook until creamy. Season to taste. The sauce can be put in a blender to make it smoother at this point, if desired. Drain salmon and place on plate and cover with sauce. Serves 4.

175

RESTAURANT ST. MICHEL'S CREPE A L'INDIENNE

2 shallots, chopped
½ stick butter
2 teaspoons curry powder
8 ounces heavy cream
4 ounces white wine
4 chicken breasts, skinned,
    deboned and diced

4 Crêpes (recipe below)
¼ cup chutney
¼ cup shredded coconut
banana, apple or mango
    slices for garnish

Sauté chopped shallots in some of the butter. Add curry powder, cream and 3 of the 4 ounces of wine. Cook the sauce 10 minutes. Sauté chicken in another pan in butter until golden. Add the curry sauce. Cook together 10 minutes, adding 1 more ounce of wine if the sauce is too thick. Reserving ¼ cup sauce, place chicken with curry sauce in the middle of each crêpe. Roll the crêpes up, place on plate, top with some of the curry sauce, and garnish with chutney, shredded coconut and fruit slices. Serves 4.

Crêpes:

2 eggs
3 ounces flour
1 to 1½ cups milk

salt and pepper to taste
(optional)

Stir the first 3 ingredients together and add salt and pepper if desired. Take ¼ cup of batter and pour onto a teflon crêpe pan, covering the surface. Cook a minute or so and flip; cook another minute. Repeat until all 4 crêpes are done.

RESTAURANT ST. MICHEL'S ESCALOPINE DE VEAU DIJONNAISE

12 2-ounce veal scallopine
½ cup flour
1 tablespoon butter, or
    more
3 ounces white wine

10 ounces heavy cream
½ cube beef bouillon
2 teaspoons Dijon mustard
4 fresh mushrooms, sliced
salt and pepper to taste

Dust veal with flour and sauté in butter for about 2 minutes. Remove from pan. Add white wine, cream, half a bouillon cube, mustard and mushrooms and reduce over heat until creamy, about 3 minutes. Add salt and pepper if desired. Add veal to sauce to reheat, then serve. Serves 4.

THE BILTMORE GRILL
Coral Gables

THE BILTMORE GRILL

For more than sixty years, the three-hundred-foot bell tower of the Biltmore Hotel has been a romantic landmark. Built by John McEntee Bowman and George Merrick, who felt his Mediterranean-style development of Coral Gables deserved a world-class hotel, the Biltmore was constructed in ten months at a cost of ten million dollars. For its January 1926 grand opening, train-loads of millionaires and celebrities came to enjoy lavish banquets, renowned orchestras, fox hunting and gondola rides.

During the 1930s the oil tycoon Henry Dougherty kept the Biltmore in the news with dazzling water shows, tea dances and golf tournaments that were frequented by Bing Crosby, Wendell Willkie, Rudy Vallee, Ginger Rogers, Judy Garland and the Duke and Duchess of Windsor.

Used as an army hospital in World War II, the hotel later became a VA hospital, with ceilings lowered, rooms partitioned and marble floors covered with linoleum. The Federal government donated it to the city of Coral Gables in 1973, and the structure sat empty for years, home only to pigeons and vagrants.

Listed on the National Register of Historic Places, the building underwent a $47 million restoration in 1986, the largest historic preservation tax act project in the state of Florida.

Since its grand reopening as a hotel in January 1987, the Biltmore has become a mecca for all those who glory in beautiful old architecture. The massive, columned lobby—with hand-painted ceilings, marble floors, mahogany paneling and a baronial fireplace—the magnificent ballrooms, the loggias overlooking the golf course and the famous pool where *Tarzan's* Johnny Weismuller once swam are all a source of much civic pride.

The Biltmore Grill, the hotel's formal dining room, is located on the ground floor, opening onto a courtyard accented with Mexican tile and a fountain. The restaurant is exquisitely elegant, with a marble entry, crystal chandeliers, gold-leafed ceilings, mirrored columns and French chairs upholstered in green velvet. The tables are comfortably spaced for privacy and are set with damask cloths, fresh flowers and silver service plates. The staff is gracious and dignified. A pianist or guitarist plays nightly.

Our meal at the Biltmore Grill began with Lightly Smoked Conch, arranged with slivers of jicama, a tasty South American vegetable, topped with a fruit dressing. The Cream of Asparagus Soup which followed was enhanced with bits of crabmeat; the Biltmore Salad was tangy and good. My entrée of Poached Maine Lobster with Mussels and Champagne Truffle Sauce was delectable. My husband Tom was thrilled with his lean, low-cholesterol Grilled Buffalo Rib-eye Steak on Smoked Corn with Garlic Cilantro Sauce. We were told that the water buffalo meat is marinated for two weeks to make it so tender and well seasoned.

As we finished our Chocolate Sacher Torte from the pastry cart, we couldn't help but rejoice that the cuisine at the Biltmore Grill is worthy of its setting.—B.R.M.

The Biltmore Grill is located on the ground floor of the Biltmore Hotel, at 1200 Anastasia Avenue in Coral Gables. It is open for dinner from 6:00 p.m. to 11:00 p.m. Tuesday through Sunday. For reservations (recommended) call (305) 445-1926.

THE BILTMORE GRILL'S COLD GREEN TOMATO SOUP WITH PASTA

12 tomatillo tomatoes (or any green tomato)
6 ounces celery
4 tablespoons clarified butter
1 onion, chopped
1 teaspoon chopped garlic
24 ounces chicken stock
1 bunch cilantro
salt and white pepper to taste
1 ounce cooked egg pasta

Remove outer skins from tomatoes; dice the tomatoes and celery. Sauté celery and tomatoes in a very hot pan with clarified butter; stir until lightly caramelized. Add onions and continue sautéing until the onions are transparent. Add garlic and cook until very light brown in color. Deglaze the pan with chicken stock; add cilantro and simmer for 30 minutes. Remove from heat and purée in blender. Pour the soup through a medium strainer. Season with salt and ground white pepper. Chill soup. Break pasta (spaghetti, noodles, linguine, etc.) into 1- inch pieces and cook according to package directions; drain. Serve soup in cold bowls, adding pasta on top at the last minute. Serves 4.

THE BILTMORE GRILL'S GULF SHRIMP ON BELGIAN ENDIVE

20 Gulf shrimp, peeled and deveined
20 Belgian endive leaves
1 carrot, julienned
1 leek, julienned
1 ounce Tosama seaweed, julienned (available at Oriental food stores)
dill leaves for garnish

Arrange endive leaves on 4 plates so that the tips are facing away from the center of the plate, symmetrically. Toss julienne of carrot, leek and seaweed together; place in the center of endive arrangement. Boil shrimp; drain and cool. Place shrimp on top of endive and spoon Shallot Poppyseed Dressing over the shrimp. Garnish with dill leaves. Serves 4.

Shallot Poppyseed Dressing:
1 tablespoon chopped shallots
2 ounces red wine vinegar
2 ounces cottonseed oil
2 teaspoons poppyseeds
1 teaspoon Pommery mustard seeds
1 teaspoon black pepper, coarsely ground
salt to taste

Mix all the ingredients well and pour over salad. Serves 4.

THE CAULEY SQUARE
TEA ROOM AND BAKERY
Goulds

THE CAULEY SQUARE TEA ROOM AND BAKERY

Far from the madding malls of Miami lies Cauley Square, a nostalgic country shopping village in South Dade.

In the early part of this century farmers and railroad workers built the cottages, barns and sheds which now house unpretentious antique, craft and specialty stores. The landmark of this ten-acre hamlet is a two-story building of stucco, coral rock and Dade County pine. It was constructed in 1920 by millionaire tomato grower William H. Cauley.

All the buildings are now owned by Mary Ann and Robert Ballard. They acquired the weathered structures over a thirty-year period with the intention of preserving them as a bit of "unsanitized" Old South Florida.

Sitting amidst unpaved roads, mango trees and native flowers is the Cauley Square Tea Room. Originally the home of the Odum family, the small, two-bedroom, concrete-block house was constructed in the 1930s and grew as the family grew.

Mary Ann Ballard opened the tea room in 1980, furnishing it with antiques from her personal collection. It is a cottage filled with delights, from butterfly collections and blooming orchids to a World War I army field stove and a Victorian baby carriage.

Adding to the warm homeyness of the tea room are the managers, Joe and Martha Wade. When Martha's son married the Ballards' daughter, Mary Ann encouraged the Wades to move from Syracuse, New York, to run the restaurant.

Martha Wade, who is originally from the Netherlands, oversees the help, coordinates the décor and serves as hostess, welcoming visitors from all over the world. Joe Wade is the cook of the family. He believes that to be successful, "You have to love your cooking. As an old Italian woman once told me, 'You add onions, garlic and a lot of love, and anything will taste good.'"

From the taste of the food served at the tea room, the love must be there. The French Onion Soup and Hot Crabmeat Au Gratin are delicious, as is the Ambrosia Salad, served with finger sandwiches made of zucchini, pumpkin and banana breads.

But the desserts are the glory of the tea room. Wonderfully rich, they are the kinds of desserts our grandmothers baked in blissful innocence of cholesterol and calories. They are desserts like Mississippi Mud Cake and old-fashioned Buttermilk, Pecan and Harvest pies. All are sinfully good. (If you want to share your guilt with family and friends, the bakery behind the restaurant enables you to buy these seducers and take them home.)—B.R.M.

The Cauley Square Tea Room and Bakery is located in Goulds, at 22400 Old Dixie Highway, two miles south of Cutler Ridge. It is open only for lunch, from 11:00 a.m. to 4:00 p.m. Monday through Saturday. It is closed Sunday and all holidays. Phone (305) 257-3725 for reservations.

CAULEY SQUARE TEA ROOM'S HARVEST PIE

8 ounces brown sugar
4 tablespoons cornstarch
pinch of salt
1 teaspoon cinnamon

6 large apples, sliced
½ bag cranberries
2 tablespoons lemon juice
1 9-inch pie shell, unbaked

Mix the first 4 dry ingredients together. Add apples, cranberries and lemon juice. Pour into an unbaked pie shell. Bake at 350 degrees for 55 to 60 minutes, or until done. When pie is cool, cover with topping.

Topping:
1 stick butter
8 ounces brown sugar
2 tablespoons evaporated
   (not condensed) milk

1 teaspoon vanilla
1 cup chopped walnuts

In a saucepan, melt the butter and cook butter and sugar for 3 minutes. Add milk, vanilla and walnuts. Spread topping over the cooled pie. Yields 1 pie.

CAULEY SQUARE TEA ROOM'S
MISSISSIPPI MUD CAKE

1 cup shortening
2 cups sugar
4 eggs
1½ cups white flour
⅓ cup cocoa

1¼ teaspoons salt
3 teaspoons vanilla
1 cup chopped walnuts
1 cup miniature
   marshmallows

Cream together the shortening and sugar. Add eggs and beat until smooth. Sift together the flour, cocoa and salt; stir into the cake mixture. Add the vanilla and walnuts. Pour into a greased 9-by-13-inch pan and bake at 300 to 320 degrees for 25 to 30 minutes. (Use a baking thermometer.) Do not overbake; the cake should appear underbaked and muddy. Remove from oven and cover with marshmallows. Return cake to oven for 5 minutes until marshmallows begin to melt. Remove and cover with aluminum foil until cool, then frost with icing. Yields 1 cake.

Icing:
1½ sticks butter
⅓ cup cocoa
1 16-ounce box confec-
   tioners' sugar

1 to 2 tablespoons canned
   milk
1 teaspoon vanilla
½ cup crushed walnuts

Melt the butter over low heat. Sift together the cocoa and confectioners' sugar. Pour butter over the dry ingredients and stir until incorporated. Add just enough canned milk to obtain a spreading consistency, then add the vanilla. Spread icing over the cake in pan and sprinkle crushed walnuts on top.

LA CONCHA RESORT HOTEL
Key West

LA CONCHA RESORT HOTEL

The six-story Hotel La Concha was the tallest and most up-to-date building in Key West when it had its grand opening in 1926. The same thing could be said of it now, after a $20 million renovation and another grand opening as the Holiday Inn La Concha Resort Hotel.

Built of stucco, with copper screens and awnings over each window, the old hotel on Duval Street was long a source of community pride. For years it hosted dances and parties and was frequented by celebrities and writers such as Ernest Hemingway, who lived in Key West for thirty years. Tennessee Williams wrote in his memoirs about staying in a "two-room suite on the top of the Hotel La Concha" with his beloved grandfather in 1946, while completing his play *A Streetcar Named Desire*.

Local residents have rejoiced to see the old hotel, which suffered years of decline and neglect, brought back to life. For the "fine rehabilitation" of the historic hotel and the "compatible new addition" that gives it more space and a pool area, the La Concha received a rehabilitation award from the Historic Florida Keys Preservation Board.

The La Concha Oyster Bar is the room most evocative of days past, with its dark wood, mirrored columns, marble floors and etched glass. In Key West tradition, it is open to the sidewalks of Duval Street, welcoming all to enjoy the live music during happy hour or to order Conch Chowder, oysters and clams or peel-your-own shrimp. At sunset, happy hour moves to the Top, the bar on the roof of La Concha, for a view of the glistening waters of the Gulf and the Atlantic and all of Key West.

More substantial fare is offered in the Rainbow Room, off the main lobby of the hotel. Done in mauve and blue tones, the room has a very stylized Art Deco look, with glass blocks accentuating a modern fountain and tall panels of glass overlooking an atrium of tropical plants.

From a menu that offered numerous salads and soups—including Chilled Gazpacho, Florida Lobster Bisque and Caribbean Black Bean Soup—and fresh seafood and beef entrées, I began with a delicious Louisiana Alligator Soup. I then enjoyed their Broiled Red Snapper Caribbean-style. The freshly made bread accompanying the meal was especially good. Never one to resist an enticing dessert, I'm glad I tried the La Concha Sand Pie.—B.R.M.

Holiday Inn La Concha Resort Hotel is located at 430 Duval Street in Key West. Breakfast hours are from 7:00 to 2:30 p.m.; lunch hours are from 11:30 a.m. to 2:30 p.m.; and dinner hours are 6:00 to 10:30 p.m. Sunday brunch is served from 11:30 a.m. to 2:30 p.m. Reservations are suggested for dinner and necessary for Sunday brunch; phone (305) 296-2991.

LA CONCHA RESORT HOTEL'S COCONUT FLAN

Caramel:

4 tablespoons cream of coconut

1½ cups sugar

Put coconut cream (a brand like Coco Lopez) and sugar in a heavy sauce pan. Stir over medium-high heat until caramelized. Pour into a 9-inch cake pan.

15 ounces sweetened condensed milk
15 ounces whole milk
4 tablespoons cream of coconut

5 eggs
1 teaspoon vanilla
1 teaspoon salt

Mix all ingredients together and strain onto the set caramel. Place cake pan in another, larger pan filled with an inch of water. Bake flan in this water bath at 350 degrees for approximately 30 minutes until set. Serves 8.

LA CONCHA RESORT HOTEL'S CONCH CHOWDER

1 pound conch meat
3 ounces salt pork
1 green pepper
4 celery stalks
1 medium onion
1 large potato
28 ounces clamatto juice
32 ounces fish stock

1 12-ounce can diced
tomatoes
2½ teaspoons Old Bay
Seasoning
1¼ teaspoons cayenne
pepper
1¼ teaspoons thyme
1 bay leaf

Sauté the conch and salt pork in a large skillet; set aside.
Dice the pepper, celery and onion; peel and dice the potato. In
a stock pot, combine clamatto juice, fish stock, diced vegetables and tomatoes. Add spices, conch and pork. Bring
chowder to a boil, then reduce heat and let simmer 1 hour.
Yields 1 gallon.

LA-TE-DA
Key West

LA-TE-DA

As I sat on the terrace of La-te-da late one weekday morning, I understood why so many people have forsaken business attire and briefcases for the tropical fantasy that is Key West. The lush palms and bougainvillea, the bubbling blue pool, the tables adorned with pink linen tablecloths and pink carnations, the waiters in pastel shirts and shorts and the classical background music create a setting of soothing beauty.

The man who orchestrated this small hotel and restaurant into a symphony of delights is owner Lawrence Formica. He was working in the construction business in Philadelphia, doing historic preservation projects, when he visited and fell in love with Key West and bought the house at 1125 Duval as his own residence. In 1977 he started renting out rooms and the hotel La Terrazo de Marti, now shortened to La-te-da, was born.

The main house of this complex was built in the late nineteenth century by Theodore Perez, while the adjoining smaller houses were constructed for cigar factory workers. Perez's friend, the Cuban poet and revolutionary Jose Marti, stayed at the house when he was exiled by the Spanish. In the early 1890s he often gave speeches from the front balcony to raise support and funds for the Cuban independence movement.

What was a scene of high adventure then is now a romantic compound of wooden-decked terraces with paddle fans, a formal interior dining room and a treehouselike dining balcony. An all-new addition to the second floor, done in a dramatic black-and-white Art Deco design, houses the Crystal Cafe, which offers small entrées and entertainment until three in the morning.

Chef Dennis O'Hara, a Kentucky native who went to the Culinary Institute of America after college, offers a wide selection of continental cuisine. Dishes include such specialties as Tortellini Martinique, Timbale of Yellowtail Snapper, lobster stuffed with a snapper mousselline, boneless breast of duckling with a grapefruit and plum sauce, Veal Zurichoise, Lamb Elizabeth and Beef Bourbon.

A combined breakfast and lunch menu is offered from nine in the morning to four in the afternoon, with a variety of interesting egg dishes, salads, seafood and meat entrées. For brunch, I enjoyed Scotch Eggs, hard-boiled eggs encased in sausage and breaded and served with Dijon mustard, mango chutney and a stunning array of fresh fruits. When the Piña Colada arrived—a frosty work of art adorned with fruit and topped with a tiny orchid—I just leaned back and reveled in the sunny charm of Key West.—B.R.M.

La-te-da is located at 1125 Duval Street in Key West. Breakfast and lunch hours are 9:00 a.m. to 4:00 p.m. Dinner is served from 4:00 p.m. to 3:00 a.m. A tea dance is held every Sunday from 5:00 to 8:00 p.m. For reservations (recommended) call (305) 294-8435.

LA-TE-DA'S BLACK OLIVE SOUP

1 pint chicken stock (or broth)
4 ounces sour cream
4 ounces yogurt
½ cucumber
½ red pepper
½ green pepper
½ cup sliced black olives
¼ cup chopped scallions
2 tablespoons chopped parsley
salt and white pepper to taste
Worcestershire sauce and Tabasco sauce to taste

Mix chicken stock, sour cream and yogurt together with a wire whip. Peel, seed and chop the cucumber and peppers. Add all the vegetables and seasonings to the sour cream mixture. Mix well. Allow to chill. Check seasonings and serve chilled. Serves 6.

LA-TE-DA'S LAMB ELIZABETH

1 rack of lamb
pinch of black pepper
¾ pound proscuitto, sliced thinly
½ pound fresh spinach, cleaned and stemmed
2 sheets of puff pastry

191

Split lamb in 2 pieces and debone it (or have this done beforehand by your grocer). Season lamb racks with black pepper. Wrap the lamb racks with the proscuitto ham, then wrap them with the fresh spinach (raw, not cooked). Lastly, wrap each piece of lamb with a sheet of 10-by-8-inch puff pastry. Bake the lamb in a preheated, 425-degree oven for approximately 25 minutes, or until the puff pastry is a golden brown. This will produce a medium-rare lamb rack. For a well-done product, bake at a lower temperature for a longer period of time. Serves 6.

LA-TE-DA'S SALAD LANDAISE

1 whole duck, roasted
1 orange
1 grapefruit
1 head lettuce (red leaf or romaine)
1 bunch watercress
¼ pound wild mushrooms (shitake)
Shallot Vinaigrette (recipe below)

Pull the meat off the duck and set it aside. Peel and divide the orange and grapefruit into sections. Chop the lettuce. Mix the duck meat with the lettuce, watercress leaves, half of the orange and grapefruit sections and the wild mushrooms. Toss with the Shallot Vinaigrette. Use the extra grapefruit and orange sections as garnish. Serves 6.

Shallot Vinaigrette:
6 tablespoons shallots, minced
2 lemons, minced
½ cup olive oil
2 tablespoons chopped parsley
2 tablespoons chopped chives
½ teaspoon salt
1 teaspoon black pepper
1 ounce Dijon mustard
1 tablespoon sugar
1 garlic clove, minced
1 cup chicken stock
½ cup peanut oil

Mix all the ingredients well, either by shaking or in a blender. Allow dressing to sit for a couple hours before serving.

192

LOUIE'S BACKYARD
Key West

LOUIE'S BACKYARD   Louie's Backyard in Key West is as big as all outdoors. It is the Atlantic Ocean, with moored sailboats. It is a sea breeze and a full moon flirting with the lapping waves. It is a terrace landscaped with sea grapes and flowers, where the aromas of good food blend with the night air.

It is the backyard of a two-story frame house, complete with front porch and rocking chairs, that was built between 1909 and 1912 by Captain James Adams, a boat builder and wrecker. In 1971, Louis Signorelli started serving dinners here, beginning with twelve a night.

Partners Proal Perry and Phil and Pat Tenney now serve one hundred and thirty to one hundred and fifty dinners nightly and have fifty-six employees. To the air-conditioned dining area of the original house, with its wooden floors and simple décor, they have added porches and terraces and decks. All overlook the water, with awnings and curtains that can be drawn to protect guests from rainshowers.

Phil Tenney, once a woodworker, built the lovely bar himself. He is supervising yet another addition; the second floor of the house is becoming a theater kitchen, where chef Norman Van Aken will create innovative specials daily. Wine tasting of expensive vintages by the glass will be another attraction.

I was at Louie's on a night in May. Torrential showers had fallen that morning; the afternoon had been sunny and hot; the evening was heaven. As we sipped the excellent house wine, Sallye Jude, an ardent preservationist who restored Island City House in Key West, recalled the last time she was at Louie's: Prince Ranier had been entertained that night at the table next to hers.

Looking over the menu, I noted that the selections were indeed fit for a king, with Wild Mushroom Pasta Timbale, Smoked Barbeque Duck with oriental noodles, Grilled Leg of Venison with red wine and mushrooms and Pan-cooked Gulf Shrimp with creole butter sauce.

As we ate a Caesar Salad with Oyster Fritters and a mixed Lettuce and Asparagus Salad with goat's cheese, Phil Tenney joined us. He confirmed the story told around town that a bartender's dog, named Ten Speed, had been a regular customer at Louie's for years, drinking a creme de noyaux—served in a champagne glass—at the bar every night. He added that when singer Jimmy Buffett once lived in the house next door, his cat Radar had also been a regular, preferring fish entrées.

While we enjoyed Roast Rack of Lamb and Norwegian Salmon with mint, cucumbers and black beans, he told us of being raised by parents who worked for the State Department and of traveling around the world. "When I saw Duval Street," he said, "I thought, *this is it*, and I stayed." His is an experience shared by many converts to the Key West life. And his restaurant might just be adding to the number of converts.—B.R.M.

Louie's Backyard is located at 700 Waddell Street in Key West. Lunch is served daily from 11:30 a.m. to 3:00 p.m., with brunch (not a buffet) on Sunday. Dinner is served from 7:00 p.m. to 11:00 p.m. in the summer, and from 6:00 p.m. to 10:30 p.m. during the season. Reservations are required; phone (305) 294-1061.

LOUIE'S BACKYARD'S HOT-FRIED CHICKEN SALAD WITH HONEY-MUSTARD DRESSING

Marinade:
2 jalapeño peppers
1½ tablespoons cayenne pepper
1½ tablespoons crushed red pepper flakes
salt and ground black pepper to taste

2 cups heavy cream
6 whole eggs
1½ tablespoons paprika
4 boneless, skinless chicken breasts

Remove stems and seeds from jalapeño peppers and cut them into thin slices. Combine jalapeños, cayenne pepper, red pepper flakes, salt and pepper, heavy cream, eggs and paprika and mix well. Cut the chicken into finger-sized pieces. Add the chicken strips to the marinade and refrigerate 12 hours or more until ready to cook.

1 head of romaine lettuce
1 head of red leaf lettuce
Honey-Mustard Dressing
   (recipe follows)
4½ cups all-purpose flour
2 tablespoons salt
6 tablespoons black pepper

9 tablespoons crushed red
   pepper flakes
3 tablespoons cayenne
   pepper
1 cup cooking oil
1 red onion, cut into rings

Wash and tear both heads of lettuce. (This can be done a few hours ahead, with the lettuce left in paper towels.) Put the salad greens in a bowl and toss with just enough dressing to lightly coat the leaves. Mound the leaves in large, chilled bowls.

Remove the chicken from the marinade, allowing the excess to drip off. Combine flour, salt, black pepper, red pepper flakes and cayenne pepper. Roll chicken in this seasoned flour. Heat oil to approximately 350 degrees. Fry the chicken, turning it from time to time until it is light brown. Remove the hot chicken to paper towels and cut into bite size pieces. Arrange the pieces over the greens and top the salad with 4 or 5 red onion rings. Serve immediately. Serves 8.

Honey-Mustard Dressing:
3 egg yolks
1½ tablespoons honey
3 ounces Creole mustard
   (or Pommery)
½ cup or less balsamic
   vinegar

1½ cups safflower oil
½ cup extravirgin olive oil
⅛ cup roasted sesame oil

Combine all the ingredients and mix well. This dressing can be made 1 or 2 days ahead of time. Serves 8.

HENRY'S AT THE CASA MARINA
Key West

HENRY'S AT THE
CASA MARINA

Henry Flagler, the millionaire visionary who brought the railroad down the east coast of Florida in the 1890s, completed his most ambitious undertaking in 1912 when he arrived on the first train to reach Key West. His Florida East Coast Railway's "Key West Extension" had just connected twenty-nine islands to the Florida mainland. It had taken seven years to complete, costing millions of dollars and hundreds of lives.

Flagler had planned to build a grand hotel in Key West, just as he had done in St. Augustine, Palm Beach and Miami. But he died in 1913, at the age of eighty-two, before seeing the realization of this last dream.

It was not until 1921 that the elegant, two-hundred-room, Spanish-Renaissance-styled Casa Marina opened. It enjoyed prosperous years in the twenties, weathered storms and the depression in the thirties and was taken over by the navy in World War II for officer housing. Then in October 1962, with the Cuban missile crisis, troops poured into Key West and the Casa Marina became the home of the Sixth Missile Battalion. Barbed wire lined its beach and, on its oceanside lawn, missiles were pointed straight at Cuba, only ninety miles away. During the late 1960s the hotel was used as a dormitory and school for the Peace Corps, and its appearance continued to deteriorate.

Finally, in 1978, massive renovations restored the Casa Marina for use as a Marriott Hotel. The lobby now gleams with its original pine floor, beamed ceiling, fireplace, arched windows and French doors. Paddle fans, plants and rattan furniture create a tropical, Old Key West ambiance.

The hotel's restaurant, Henry's, is named in honor of Henry Flagler. It is much the same as it was in the 1920s, though extra dining levels have been added, complete with wooden, trellislike gazebos.

In the evening, waiters wear black tuxedos. A pianist plays for diners who enjoy specials ranging from a delicious Blackened Key West Yellowtail to Rack of Lamb, Prime Rib and Veal Piccata.

A rich array of desserts—like Key Lime Pie, Sabayon and Flambéed Jamaican Bananas—is offered, as are exotic coffees. I personally couldn't resist the Macadamia Nut Chocolate Cream Cheese Pie.

On Sunday, as is traditional in Key West, a big brunch is served out on the veranda overlooking the Atlantic.—B.R.M.

Henry's is located in the Casa Marina Resort on Reynolds Street on the ocean in Key West. Breakfast is served daily from 7:30 a.m. to 11:00 a.m. Lunch is served from 11:30 a.m. to 2:00 p.m. each day except Sunday, when brunch is served from 10:00 a.m. until 2:00 p.m. Dinner is served from 6:00 p.m. to 10:00 p.m. on weekdays, and until 11:00 p.m. on Friday and Saturday. Reservations are suggested; call (305) 296-3535.

HENRY'S MACADAMIA NUT CHOCOLATE CREAM CHEESE PIE

Pie Shell:

½ package Oreo cookies, crushed

6 tablespoons melted butter

3 ounces macadamia nuts, finely chopped

Mix all the ingredients together. Using the back of a spoon or your fingers, press the mixture against the bottom and sides of a 9-inch pie plate. Bake in a 350-degree oven for 5 minutes. Cool.

Filling:

8 ounces cream cheese
6 ounces sugar
2 teaspoons vanilla
2 egg yolks
6 ounces semisweet choco-
late, melted

4 egg whites
6 ounces macadamia nuts, chopped
16 ounces whipped dairy topping

Mix cream cheese, 4 ounces of the sugar and vanilla in a blender or with an electric mixer until smooth. To this mixture, slowly add egg yolks and melted chocolate and blend until smooth. Set aside. Whip egg whites and 2 ounces of

199

sugar into a meringue. Fold chocolate mixture into meringue. Fold in macadamia nuts, then dairy topping. Refrigerate until mixture sets up, then spoon into cooled pie shell. Serves 6 to 8.

HENRY'S CAESAR SALAD

2 small garlic cloves
3 anchovy fillets
4 tablespoons olive oil
1 teaspoon Dijon mustard
dash of Worcestershire
  sauce
1 tablespoon wine vinegar

1 coddled egg (heated for 1
  minute)
½ lemon
8 ounces romaine lettuce
¼ cup Parmesan cheese
fresh pepper to taste
½ cup croutons

Crush garlic cloves and rub garlic over a large salad bowl; remove the remains. In the salad bowl, crush the anchovies with a fork into a paste, and add 1 tablespoon of the olive oil. Add the mustard, Worcestershire sauce, 3 tablespoons of olive oil and the wine vinegar. Break a coddled egg into the mixture and blend. Wrap the lemon in a cheesecloth, squeeze lemon into the mixture and blend. Add romaine lettuce and toss. Sprinkle Parmesan cheese over top and grind on some pepper. Add croutons and toss. Serve on chilled plates. Serves 2.

HENRY'S BLACKENED KEY WEST YELLOWTAIL

1 tablespoon sweet paprika
2½ teaspoons salt
1 teaspoon onion powder
1 teaspoon garlic powder
1 teaspoon cayenne pepper
1 teaspoon white pepper
1 teaspoon black pepper

½ teaspoon dried thyme
  leaves
½ teaspoon dried oregano
  leaves
6 10-ounce yellowtail
  fillets
1 stick butter, melted

Thoroughly combine the seasonings in a bowl. Dip each fillet into melted butter and sprinkle the seasoning mix on generously. Heat a cast-iron skillet until extremely hot. Place fillets in the hot skillet and cook until the seasoning mix on the fish looks charred. Turn fillets over and repeat the process. Pour a small amount of butter over the fillets and continue cooking until fillets are firm. Serves 6.

INDEX

ENTREES

Fowl:

Meats:

Pasta:

Seafood:

Pompano aux Pecans, La
Vieille Maîson 148
Red Snapper Bretonne, Park
Plaza Gardens 80
Salade de Homard aux Truffles
et Caviar, King Charles 116
Salmon Croquettes, Primrose
Inn 55
Salmon with Ginger Cream
Sauce, Restaurant St.
Michel 175
Sautéed Conch Steaks with
Lime Butter and Sautéed
Almonds, Tobacco Road 168
Sautéed Shrimp and Scallops
sur Lit d'Epinard,
Charade 172
Scallops Sauté, 1912 the
Restaurant 19
Seafood Jambalaya, Kacin's
Casablanca Cafe 103
Shrimp Anderson, Sovereign
Restaurant 59
Shrimp Creole, Santa Maria 44
Shrimp de Jongue, Old Cap-
tiva House 131
Shrimp Riviera, Casa
Vecchia 159
Shrimp Tempura, The
Breakers 143
Snapper Alicante,
Columbia 99
Sole Marschel, Pelican
Restaurant 140
Stone Crab Croquettes, King's
Crown Dining Room 128
Swordfish in Pineapple Tar-
ragon Sauce, Raintree
Restaurant 48
Trota ala Primavera (Trout
Primavera), Casa Vecchia 160

SALADS
Caesar Salad, Henry's 200
Chicken, Avocado and Bacon

Salad, Lili Marlene's Aviators
Pub and Restaurant 83
Chicken Salad, Palace
Saloon 36
Chicken Walnut Salad, First
and Broadway 68
Gulf Shrimp on Belgian
Endive, Biltmore Grill 180
Hot-Fried Chicken Salad,
Louie's Backyard 195
Salade de Homard aux Truffles
et Caviar, King Charles 116
Salade Floridienne, La Vieille
Maîson 147
Salad Landaise, La-te-da 192
Tuna Salad, Palace Saloon 35

**SAUCES, GRAVIES AND
DRESSINGS**
Athenian Sauce, Siple's Garden
Seat 107
Béarnaise Sauce, Belleview
Biltmore 112
Béarnaise Sauce, Pelican
Restaurant 140
Brown Sauce, 1878 Steak
House 31
Cocktail Sauce, Perry's Seafood
House 8
Cornish Game Hen Dressing,
Wakulla Springs Lodge 27
Dijon Sauce, Cap's Place 151
Ginger Cream Sauce, Restau-
rant St. Michel 175
Honey-Mustard Dressing,
Louie's Backyard 196
House Dressing, Belleview
Biltmore 111
House Dressing, Cabbage Key
Inn 124
Key Lime Butter, King's Crown
Dining Room 127
Melba Sauce, 1878 Steak
House 32

203

Muscatel Wine Sauce, Golden
Pheasant 24
Mustard Sauce, Joe's Stone
Crab 164
Pesto Sauce, First and
Broadway 67
Pommery Sauce, King's Crown
Dining Room 128
Raspberry Vinaigrette Dressing, Lili Marlene's Aviators
Pub and Restaurant 84
Remoulade Sauce, Perry's Seafood House 8
Roasted Red Pepper and
Saffron Sauce, Jamie's French
Restaurant 16
Salad Dressing, King
Charles 116
Shallot Poppyseed Dressing,
Biltmore Grill 180
Shallot Vinaigrette, La-te-da 192
Tarragon Dressing, Lili Marlene's Aviators Pub and
Restaurant 83
Tofu Salad Dressing, Great
Outdoors Cafe 51
Vinaigrette Salad Dressing,
Joe's Stone Crab 163

SOUPS AND CHOWDERS
Black Bean, Santa Maria 43
Black Olive Soup, La-te-da 191
Caldo Gallego, Valencia
Garden 96
Cantaloupe Supreme, Belleview Biltmore 111
Chili, Coley's 119
Clam Chowder, Great Outdoors Cafe 52
Claude's Bouillabaise, Le
Pavillon 40
Cold Avocado Soup, Jamie's
French Restaurant 16
Cold Green Tomato Soup,
Biltmore Grill 179

Conch Chowder, La Concha
Resort Hotel 188
Gratinée au Brie, La Belle
Verrière 75
Navy Bean Soup, Wakulla
Springs Lodge 28
Peaches and Cream Soup,
Lakeside Inn 72

VEGETABLES
Cottage Fried Sweet Potatoes,
Joe's Stone Crab 163
Grilled Tomatoes, Joe's Stone
Crab 164
Squash Casserole, Primrose
Inn 55
Squash Soufflé, Reececliff 91
Stewed Okra and Tomatoes,
Hopkins Boarding House 11
Stuffed Eggplant, Scotto's
Ristorante Italiano 3
Sweet Potato Soufflé, Hopkins
Boarding House 11
Vegetable Napolean,
Veranda 135